Advanced Introduction to International Political Economy

Elgar Advanced Introductions are stimulating and thoughtful introductions to major fields in the social sciences and law, expertly written by some of the world's leading scholars. Designed to be accessible yet rigorous, they offer concise and lucid surveys of the substantive and policy issues associated with discrete subject areas.

The aims of the series are two-fold: to pinpoint essential principles of a particular field, and to offer insights that stimulate critical thinking. By distilling the vast and often technical corpus of information on the subject into a concise and meaningful form, the books serve as accessible introductions for undergraduate and graduate students coming to the subject for the first time. Importantly, they also develop well-informed, nuanced critiques of the field that will challenge and extend the understanding of advanced students, scholars and policy-makers.

Titles in the series include:

International Political Economy
Benjamin J. Cohen

The Austrian School of Economics
Randall G. Holcombe

International Conflict and Security Law
Nigel D. White

Comparative Constitutional Law
Mark Tushnet

Advanced Introduction to

International Political Economy

BENJAMIN J. COHEN

Louis G. Lancaster Professor of International Political Economy, University of California, Santa Barbara, USA

Elgar Advanced Introductions

Edward Elgar
Cheltenham, UK • Northampton, MA, USA

Published by
Edward Elgar Publishing Limited
The Lypiatts
15 Lansdown Road
Cheltenham
Glos GL50 2JA
UK

Edward Elgar Publishing, Inc.
William Pratt House
9 Dewey Court
Northampton
Massachusetts 01060
USA

A catalogue record for this book
is available from the British Library
Library of Congress Control Number: 2013949814

This book is available electronically in the ElgarOnline.com
Social and Political Science Subject Collection, E-ISBN 978 1 78195 156 9

ISBN 978 1 78195 155 2 (cased)
ISBN 978 1 78195 157 6 (paperback)

Typeset by Servis Filmsetting Ltd, Stockport, Cheshire
Printed and bound in Great Britain by T.J. International Ltd, Padstow

For Jane
Once again, with even more feeling

Contents

Acknowledgements

This book could not have been written without the help of literally dozens of friends and colleagues around the world. I am deeply grateful to them all for their willingness to take the time to answer my questions and provide information in private communications.

I am especially grateful to the following individuals who provided me with valuable comments on some or all of the manuscript as it was being drafted: Richard Appelbaum, Mark Brawley, Greg Chin, Kevin Gallagher, Randy Germain, Jean-Christophe Graz, Eric Helleiner, Eric Hershberg, David Lake, Susanne Lütz, Craig Murphy, Andreas Nölke, Lou Pauly, Nicola Phillips, John Ravenhill, Leonard Seabrooke, Jason Sharman, Diana Tussie, Geoffrey Underhill, Hongying Wang, Wang Yong, and Hubert Zimmerman. I will forever remain in their debt, although of course the usual disclaimer applies. I alone remain responsible for any remaining errors or omissions.

I am also deeply grateful to several of my students for their research assistance, including Michael Albert, Geoff Allen, Tabitha Benney, and Tian Wu.

Finally, this book is dedicated to my wife, Jane De Hart – once again, with even more feeling.

Abbreviations

AEA	American Economic Association
APSA	American Political Science Association
BISA	British International Studies Association
BRIC	Brazil, Russia, India, China
CEPAL	Economic Commission for Latin America and the Caribbean (also ECLAC)
CPE	comparative political economy
ECLAC	Economic Commission for Latin America and the Caribbean (also CEPAL)
ECPR	European Consortium for Political Research
EIPE	Everyday International Political Economy
EISA	European International Studies Association
EPER	*European Political Economy Review*
EPIC	European Political Economy Infrastructure Consortium
FLACSO	Latin American School of Social Sciences
GPE	global political economy
HST	hegemonic stability theory
IPE	international political economy
IPEG	International Political Economy Group
IPES	International Political Economy Society
IR	international relations
ISA	International Studies Association
ISI	import substitution industrialization
IWEP	Institute of World Economics and Politics
LATN	Latin American Trade Network
OEP	open economy politics
TRIP	Teaching, Research, and International Policy project
US	United States

1 Introduction

What is International Political Economy (IPE)? Even for an advanced student, that is not an easy question to answer. Clearly, IPE has something to do with economics (economy). It also has something to do with politics (political). And it somehow relates to the world beyond the confines of the individual state (international). On these three elements, all scholars concur. However, that is about as far as agreement reaches. In practice, there seem to be almost as many conceptions of IPE as there are specialists in the field. As one expert wearily concedes, IPE is "a notoriously diverse field of study" (Payne 2005: 69). A second simply calls it "schizoid" (Underhill 2000: 806).

Among possible definitions, my personal favorite comes from Robert Gilpin, one of the pioneers of IPE in the United States. International political economy, he suggested, may be thought of as "the reciprocal and dynamic interaction in international relations of the pursuit of wealth and the pursuit of power" (Gilpin 1975: 43). By pursuit of wealth, Gilpin had in mind the realm of economics: the role of markets and other allocative mechanisms and the challenges of providing for material welfare, which are among the central concerns of economists. By pursuit of power, he had in mind the realm of politics: the role of the state and other political actors and the challenges of effective governance, which are among the central concerns of political scientists. By international relations he meant actions and outcomes that extend across national frontiers, which are among the central concerns of students of international or global affairs. By reciprocal he meant that neither economics nor politics takes precedence: each influences and, in turn, is influenced by the other. And by dynamic he meant that nothing can be taken for granted: things change. To a remarkable degree, this concise definition captures what IPE is all about.

One point of confusion stems from the seeming overlap between IPE and the closely related specialty of *comparative* political economy (CPE). Like IPE, CPE involves reciprocal and dynamic interactions between the realms of economics and politics. Unlike IPE, however, CPE tends to discount the international, which is a critical part of Gilpin's definition. In CPE, the emphasis is more on what goes on *within* national units – the making of policy, the evolution of institutions, and the like. National units are compared and contrasted for their similarities and differences. In IPE, by contrast, the emphasis is on what goes on *between* national units – the linkages created by trade, finance and other types of cross-border relationships. The two fields, clearly, share much in common; indeed, specialists in either field may at times find themselves doing work that is more in the tradition of the other. Nonetheless, the distinction between the two disciplines is vital. What distinguishes IPE is the first word – *international.*

Following standard practice, the term IPE (or the capitalized words International Political Economy) will be used here to refer to the field of study that is the subject of this *Advanced Introduction.* The same meaning will also be attached to the term Global Political Economy (GPE), a frequently used synonym for the field. Without capital letters, international or global political economy may be understood to refer to the material world – the myriad connections between economics and politics across the globe that we read about in the daily newspaper or on our favorite blog.

History

As a field of study, IPE is both very old and very young. It is old because the connections between economics and politics in international relations have long been recognized and explored by keen observers. However, it is also young because, until recently, it had not yet achieved the status of a formal, established academic discipline. The modern field of IPE, as we know it today, has actually been in existence for less than half a century.

A formal field of study may be said to exist when a coherent body of knowledge is developed to define a subject of inquiry. Recognized standards come to be employed to train and certify specialists; full-time employment opportunities become available in university teaching and research; professional associations are established to promote study and dialogue; and publishing venues become available to help disseminate new ideas and analysis. In short, an institutionalized network of scholars comes into being, a distinct research community with its own boundaries, rewards and careers – an "invisible college," as it is sometimes called. In IPE, the invisible college did not begin to coalesce until around the end of the 1960s.

There were precursors, of course. In terms of intellectual antecedents, today's field actually has a long and distinguished lineage, going back to the liberal Enlightenment that spread across Europe in the seventeenth and eighteenth centuries. Even before there were separate disciplines of economics and political science, there was classical political economy – the label given to the study of economic aspects of public policy. Classical political economy encompassed three broad discourses: a practical discourse about policy, a normative discourse about the ideal relationship between the state and the economy, and a scientific discourse about the way the economy operates as a social system (Gamble 1995). All three discourses were key inspirations for today's invisible college. A recent commentary is correct in insisting that "IPE did not undergo a pure virgin birth ... without classical political economy there could be no modern IPE" (Hobson 2013).

Classical political economy flourished through the eighteenth and early nineteenth centuries. From the French physiocrats and Adam Smith onward, the classical political economists all understood their subject to be a unified social science closely linked to the study of moral philosophy. Their perspective was self-consciously broad and inclusive. "The classical political economists were polymaths, who wrote on a variety of subjects," one expert has written (Watson 2005: 18). "They did not study 'the economy' as an enclosed and self-contained entity." The earliest university departments teaching the subject were all designated departments of political economy. John Stuart Mill's monumental summary of all economic knowledge in the mid-nineteenth century was pointedly entitled *Principles of Political Economy*.

Not long after Mill, however, a split began, fragmenting the social sciences in many parts of the world. Like an amoeba, classical political economy started to subdivide. In place of the earlier conception of a unified economic and political order, two separate realms were envisioned, representing two distinct spheres of human activity. One was "society," the private sector, based on contracts and decentralized market activity and concerned largely with issues of production and distribution. The other was the "state," the public sector, based on coercive authority and concerned with power, collective decision-making, and the resolution of conflict. Many university departments were systematically reorganized to address the divergent agendas of the two realms. By the start of the twentieth century, the divorce of political science from economics was well underway, with fewer and fewer points of intellectual contact or communication remaining between them.

Not everyone elected to choose sides. In many places, particularly in Continental Europe and Latin America, the tradition of classical political economy lingered on. The split was deepest in the United States and Britain, where only a few hardy souls continued to stress links between the pursuit of wealth and the pursuit of power. Most were to be found at the radical fringes of US and British academia, heterodox observers outside the "respectable" mainstream of scholarship. These included Marxist or neo-Marxist circles on the Left, where the superstructure of politics was unquestioningly assumed to rest on a foundation defined by prevailing modes of production, as well as *laissez-faire* liberals or libertarians on the Right determined to preserve capitalism against the oppressive power of the state. There were also some notable exceptions closer to the orthodox mainstream in both countries. One was the great British economist John Maynard Keynes, who cared deeply about the relationship between markets and politics. Another was Joseph Schumpeter, an Austrian polymath who taught for many years at Harvard, best known for his magisterial treatise on *Capitalism, Socialism and Democracy* (1942). A third was Jacob Viner, a Canadian economist transplanted to the United States. Long before Gilpin, Viner (1948) had already remarked on the interaction between "power" and "plenty" in the foreign economic policies of nations, dating back to the era of Mercantilism in the seventeenth and eighteenth centuries.

For the most part, however, the void only grew deeper with time, especially among students of world affairs. References to political economy at the international level soon disappeared from polite conversation. By mid-twentieth century, in most places, the frontier dividing the economics and politics of global affairs had become firm and seemingly impassable. Scholars working in the separate specialties of international economics and international relations (IR) simply did not speak to one another. It was like a dialogue of the deaf.

The dichotomy was summarized acutely in a seminal article published in 1970 by British scholar Susan Strange, provocatively entitled "International economics and international relations: a case of mutual neglect" (Strange 1970). The void between international economics and IR had endured for too long, Strange declared. Scholars from both traditions were neglecting fundamental changes in the world economy. The dialogue of the deaf should not be allowed to persist. A more modern approach to the study of international economic relations was needed – a determined effort at "bridge-building" to spotlight the crucial "middle ground" between economic and political analysis of international affairs. Here, for the first time, was a full and compelling case laid out for a new field of study, a clarion call expressed in the fierce and uncompromising manner that came to be Strange's trademark. The article was, for all intents and purposes, a manifesto.

Strange's summons to battle was by no means the sole spark to ignite a renewed interest in the political economy of international relations. By 1970, there were also others – principally in Britain and the United States – who were beginning to grope their way toward reconnecting the two realms of inquiry, "reintegrating what had been somewhat arbitrarily split up" (Underhill 2000: 808). Yet looking back, we can now appreciate how significant her manifesto was. Its publication marked something of a tipping point. Never before had the brewing discontent among scholars been so effectively distilled and bottled. Nowhere else had the issue been posed in such concise and focused terms. As such, it is as good a candidate as any to mark the moment of birth of the modern field of IPE.

In an earlier book, *International Political Economy: An Intellectual History* (Cohen 2008), I provided a brief history of the field since the early 1970s. The coverage of that volume was deliberately limited to the English-speaking world – often called the "Anglosphere" – defined to include mainly the United States, Canada, the British Isles, and the Antipodes. It was also limited to what might be considered mainstream conceptions of IPE in the Anglosphere, excluding outliers. Although my intention was to broaden horizons by going beyond a single orthodoxy, the book was nonetheless criticized for being unduly narrow in its coverage. In the words of one commentator, "Cohen's account excludes too much . . . These exclusions amount to omitting a considerable part of what is taught and written in IPE" (Leander 2009: 322–323). As it happens, I agree – hence this *Advanced Introduction*, which may be considered something of a sequel to my earlier *Intellectual History*. This book takes us much further afield, broadening horizons even more. My aim is to provide a comprehensive *tour d'horizon* of IPE as it exists today across the globe.

Diversity

Since the early 1970s, an invisible college has coalesced around the subject of IPE. However, the community is hardly monolithic. Bridges have been built, as Strange urged, to span the void between international economics and IR. Yet the connections have been many and varied, offering a colorful array of alternative perspectives. Once born, the modern field proceeded to develop along sharply divergent paths followed by different clusters of scholars. Although united by a shared purpose – a determination to overcome the dialogue of the deaf between economists and political scientists – the invisible college also divided into contending, and occasionally warring, factions.

A faction may be understood to denote a group of scholars with a shared understanding of broad basics. It does not demand agreement on specific goals or one single research agenda. A synonymous term is "school of thought." The development of factions or schools is hardly unfamiliar in academic life, as the philosopher of science Thomas Kuhn (1962) long ago pointed out. Research specialties commonly subdivide as experts seek out the comfort of others who share the same values and assumptions. In the words of political psychologist Margaret Hermann (1998: 606), "Our identities become intertwined with the perspectives and points of view of the theoretical cohort to which we perceive ourselves belonging. And we tend to distance ourselves from those we do not understand or whose ideas seem discordant with our group's theoretical outlook." Differences then tend to be reinforced over time by divergent patterns of professional socialization, producing what the sociology of science calls distinct "discourse coalitions" (Wæver 1998). The emergence of factions within the invisible college is an altogether natural process.

Nor is it necessarily a bad thing, so long as the diverse schools encourage a lively competition of ideas. A research community without factions is like a monoculture in farming, dominated by a single biological species. Agricultural monocultures, it is known, can be highly efficient, since there is less unpredictability in cultivation and no need for trial and error. Similarly, in an academic monoculture, no time need be wasted arguing about basic standards or methodologies. However, as political scientist Kathleeen McNamara (2011: 65, 70) has reminded us, "monocultures, be they intellectual or agricultural, are never healthy . . . Intellectual monocultures, where one theoretical perspective, ontological position, and method are used exclusively, may well result in a . . . desiccation of the field of study." Scholarship becomes arid and offers diminishing returns. The emergence of factions, like the cultivation of diverse crops, can help to preserve a field's fertility.

Much depends, however, on the degree of communication between the factions: how well acquainted discourse coalitions are with each other and how open they are to alternative points of view. Are they willing to learn from one another? Are they even aware of the existence of other schools? The kind of socialization that Hermann (1998) talks about can build up a powerful momentum of its own. Cohorts may begin to distance themselves so much that they become effectively insular, if not isolated, foregoing the benefits of cross-fertilization. New dialogues of the deaf emerge. That is what happened to the classical political economy of the Enlightenment, when economists and political scientists stopped talking to each other. It can in fact happen to any academic specialty – including IPE.

Indeed, the field of IPE today would seem to be at particular risk, judging from the way the subject is typically taught in many places around the world. Too often, in course syllabi and lectures, students are mainly exposed to just a single version of IPE – something approaching a monoculture in miniature. Students may believe that they are joining a broad invisible college. In fact, without even knowing it, many instead are being initiated into a more narrow faction, trained to remain loyal to one tradition among many. Consciously or unconsciously, they become members of a single discourse coalition, and insularity is reinforced.

Why worry, some might ask. At least students are acquiring some grasp of the field, even if not the whole picture. Yet that way lies misconception and a potentially distorted perception of reality. As an old Yiddish saying puts it, a half-truth is a whole lie. Students deserve the whole truth. To get it, they must be reminded that there are in fact multiple versions of IPE, each with its own distinct personality. They must be shown that much can be learned from every faction. That is the central purpose of this *Advanced Introduction*.

Factions

Who are these factions, and what distinguishes them? Beyond the bridges built to span the void between international economics and IR, specialists in IPE can – and do – divide over a number of critical points of substance or style. Five dimensions stand out:

(1) *Ontology*. From the Greek for "things that exist," ontology is about investigating reality: the nature, essential properties, and relations of being. What are the basic units of analysis in our research, and what are their key relationships? Do we primarily study individuals, enterprises, social units, sovereign states, or the "system" as a whole?

(2) *Agenda*. What are the most salient issues to be addressed? Are we more interested in matters relating to material welfare – the production and distribution of goods and services for final use – as emphasized by the discipline of economics? Or is our interest more in issues of politics and governance – decision-making, cooperation, and the management of conflict – as stressed by political scientists? Are our horizons primarily local or regional, or does our perspective extend to the intercontinental and global?

(3) *Purpose*. What is the goal of research? Is our aim "positive," intended primarily to enhance our objective understanding of how the world works? Or, rather, is it more "normative," hoping to make the world a better place to live?

(4) *Openness*. How receptive are we to ideas or insights from other disciplines beyond economics and political science? How important are related specialties like sociology, anthropology, history, geography, or psychology? And what about other more distant specialties such as law, philosophy, religion, or even cultural or gender studies?

(5) *Epistemology*. From the Greek word for "knowledge," epistemology has to do with the methods and grounds of knowing. What methodologies do we use to study the world? What kinds of analytical techniques will best enhance our understanding?

We know that differences exist in all these dimensions. It is not always easy, however, to know where to draw the lines. Any set of labels to categorize factions is bound in some degree to be arbitrary – and therefore controversial. Alternative traditions may diverge along some dimensions even while converging on others; elements of several versions may overlap and intertwine, even in the minds of individual scholars.

The world of scholarship is inherently messy, a raucous cacophony of voices competing for attention. No one system of classification can possibly do justice to them all.

Some differences, however, are more readily apparent than others – and, arguably, the most obvious differences tend to be *geographic*: national or, in some cases, regional (encompassing a number of neighboring nations). Not all experts agree. According to the Canadian Tony Porter (2001), "it is only minimally useful to speak about 'national perspectives' on international relations." The weight of the evidence, however, suggests otherwise. Clustering comes naturally to citizens of the same nation, who more often than not share a common language, attend the same schools, join the same associations, read the same journals, and have less distance to travel in order to talk with one another – all influences that act as centripetal forces to differentiate one national tradition from others. The same can also be said of certain multistate regions, such as Latin America. The sociology of science recognizes that there really are basic differences in intellectual cultures across the globe, shaped by the unique history, language, institutions, and politics of individual countries or regions. These cultural differences are paramount in determining how most scholars see the world, particularly in the social sciences (Wæver 1998).

Moreover, once differences like these begin to assert themselves, they tend to be replicated and strongly reinforced through the training and advancement of successive generations of scholars – what one source (Biersteker 2009: 310) calls "practices of intellectual reproduction." University departments, in particular, play a crucial gatekeeping role. They decide what courses will be taught, who will fill faculty vacancies, and who will be promoted or granted tenure. Funding sources decide whose research will be supported. Program chairs decide what work will be featured at professional meetings. Journal editors and book publishers decide which scholarship will appear in print. In very tangible ways, all these practices serve to define and perpetuate distinctive schools of thought.

As a first approximation, therefore, it does not seem unreasonable to start with geography to define the principal factions in IPE. That is the approach that I took in my *Intellectual History*, where across the Anglosphere I spotlighted a deep and abiding schism that I called the transatlantic divide (Cohen 2007). The transatlantic divide, I argued, separates two starkly different conceptions of IPE: an American school and a British school. The line between the two schools, in my view, reflected above all a basic contrast in intellectual cultures – broadly, the way the subject of international studies traditionally has been approached in universities on either side of the Atlantic. On the American side of the "pond," links with political science have always dominated. International studies grew up in an environment framed by the norms of conventional US social science, with a particular emphasis on positivist analysis and training in quantitative methods. Once modern IPE was born, it seemed natural for most American scholars to channel the infant field's development along similar lines. In Britain, by contrast, training in international studies has roots that are spread much more widely into a variety of other disciplines, including especially sociology, history, and law. Direct links with political science have always tended to be weaker, with most universities maintaining a strong institutional separation between IR faculty and others. British academics were already conditioned to think about the international realm in multidisciplinary fashion. Hence it was no surprise that in Britain the new field of IPE might develop in the same open manner.

By extension, geography is the approach that I use in this *Advanced Introduction* as well. The idea is to give students a sense of the remarkably wide range of approaches to IPE that can be found around the globe. Coverage is limited to those parts of the world where a "critical mass" of scholars has managed to come together to form a distinct research community. Readers may wonder why there is no chapter on Russia or Japan or the Arab world or Africa. Certainly, in many of these places, one or a few individuals may be seen doing work that is recognizably IPE in nature. However, they are not included here because their numbers are simply too small to form a genuinely distinctive discourse coalition. Beyond the Anglosphere, local versions of the field are still mostly at an earlier stage of development. In many countries or regions, the formation of an institutionalized network of scholars has barely even begun.

I start with the American and British schools, the two sides of the transatlantic divide, since it was in the United States and Britain that the modern field of IPE first began to take shape. These two countries are home to the most established factions of the invisible college, complete with their own professional associations, numerous employment opportunities, and respected publishing venues. After taking due account of competing alternatives to be found elsewhere in the English-speaking world, I will then move on to national and regional traditions in other languages, focusing in particular on the European continent, Latin America, and China. The penultimate chapter will take a look at how the different communities fit together and relate to one another – a sketch of what we may call the geography of IPE. The book will then conclude with a brief discussion of what we have learned from all these diverse efforts.

Limits

Geographic labels have their limits, of course. "Typologies are most useful," the noted scholar John Ravenhill (2008: 26) has reminded us, "when they have minimal within-type variance and maximum between-type variation." The geographic approach that I propose here has been roundly criticized by many (including Ravenhill) for failing to meet these criteria. On the one hand, even within a single country or region, there are bound to be significant differences. Despite all that US scholars share in common, for instance, the American school rarely speaks with one voice. Even within the US-based research community, diverse camps have emerged over time, making for lively debate and a cross-fertilization of ideas. I acknowledged as much in an essay written after my *Intellectual History*, entitled "The multiple traditions of American IPE" (Cohen 2009), and will have more to say about that in the next chapter. No national or regional faction can be expected to be totally without some degree of within-type variance.

On the other hand, even for a single faction, adherence may well be much broader than a single country or region. Certainly there are many outside the United States who proudly identify themselves with the tenets of the American school despite their residence elsewhere. Not surprisingly, that tends to be especially true of scholars who trained in US universities. Conversely, as I wrote in my *Intellectual History*, you do not have to be British to be in the British school; you do not even have to live in Britain. No faction should be assumed to be strictly confined to a single country or region either. Some muddling of between-type variation is to be expected too.

Migration, in particular, tends to blur the lines between factions. Academics move around, and when they do they bring new elements that may shake up older traditions. Ravenhill is a case in point – originally a Briton who has shifted back and forth between British and Australian universities and most recently has relocated to Canada.

Other examples include Geoffrey Underhill, a Canadian long based in the Netherlands, and Leonard Seabrooke, an Australian who teaches in Denmark. Transplants like these tend both to increase within-type variance and decrease between-type variation.

Yet what else is there? It is easy to find fault with a geographic approach to categorization of the field. It is harder to find something better.

Some critics just throw up their hands, in effect overwhelmed by the notorious diversity of the field. Typical is the Norwegian Helge Hveem (2011), who questions whether one should even try to think in terms of schools in IPE. The field, he argues, is simply too much of a *pot pourri* to capture in any single system of classification. I can sympathize with Hveem's frustration, but as an educator I regard his advice as an abject surrender of responsibility. Students deserve more clarity than that.

Others go to the opposite extreme, producing taxonomies of such density that they make the eyes glaze over. A representative example is offered by Matthew Watson (2011), an accomplished historian of IPE. Starting with a simple two-by-two matrix, Watson ultimately identifies some 19 separate "traditions of thought" intricately connected to one another by one or more degrees of separation in a complex web of relationships. One can admire the erudition underlying such an approach, yet question its usefulness. The purpose of any typology should be to simplify and clarify, not overwhelm.

Between these extremes yet others have proposed various dichotomies in the field, such as orthodox/heterodox or positivist/critical or rationalist/nonrationalist. Most such dualities can be considered variations of a theme first struck years ago by one of the doyens of the British school, Robert Cox (1981), who distinguished between what he called "problem-solving theory" and "critical theory" in IPE. (More on that later.) Pairings like these provide much insight and certainly maximize between-type variation but still leave us with an enormous amount of within-type variance.

Perhaps the most popular alternative to a geographic approach is a strategy first proposed by Gilpin back in the field's early years. Three schools of thought could be identified, he averred, all drawn from traditional IR theory – liberalism, Marxism, and realism – each offering students of IPE its own distinct "model of the future" (Gilpin 1975). The advantage of the strategy was that for many it facilitated an organic construction of the new field of study on familiar foundations provided by political science. Even now, Gilpin's three "models" – frequently also referred to as paradigms or perspectives – remain a staple of many introductory textbooks, especially in the United States. The biggest disadvantage is that over time, as the field has evolved around the world, diverse alternative perspectives have emerged that do not fit comfortably into any one of Gilpin's three models. Where do we place constructivism, for instance, or the various versions of critical theory? In many textbooks today, one finds as much space allocated to alternatives to the three models as to the models themselves. Gilpin's trichotomy, useful as it was as a starting point in IPE's infancy, simply cannot claim to encompass the full breadth and complexity of the field as it exists today.

For all their limits, therefore, geographic labels still seem to provide the most helpful principle for organizing a comprehensive introduction to today's many versions of IPE. The approach is accessible and easy to follow, yet informative, and does minimal violence to reality. Advanced students deserve to be informed about the full array of perspectives to be found across the globe in this rich field of study.

References

Biersteker, Thomas J. (2009), "The parochialism of hegemony: challenges for 'American' international relations," in Arlene B. Tickner and Ole Wæver (eds), *International Relations Scholarship Around the World*, London: Routledge, pp. 308–327.

Cohen, Benjamin J. (2007), "The transatlantic divide: why are American and British IPE so different?," *Review of International Political Economy*, **14** (2), 197–219.

Cohen, Benjamin J. (2008), *International Political Economy: An Intellectual History*, Princeton, NJ: Princeton University Press.

Cohen, Benjamin J. (2009), "The multiple traditions of American IPE," in Mark Blyth (ed.), *Routledge Handbook of International Political Economy (IPE): IPE as a Global Conversation*, London: Routledge, pp. 23–35.

Cox, Robert W. (1981), "Social forces, states, and world orders: beyond international relations theory," *Millennium*, **10** (2), 126–155.

Gamble, Andrew (1995), "The new political economy," *Political Studies*, **43** (3), 516–530.

Gilpin, Robert (1975), *U.S. Power and the Multinational Corporation*, New York: Basic Books.

Hermann, Margaret (1998), "One field, many perspectives: building the foundations for dialogue," *International Studies Quarterly*, **42** (4), 605–624.

Hobson, John M. (2013), "Part I – revealing the Eurocentric foundations of IPE: a critical historiography of the discipline from the classical to the modern era," *Review of International Political Economy*, **20** (5), in press.

Hveem, Helge (2011), "Pluralist IPE: a view from outside the 'schools,'" in Nicola Phillips and Catherine E. Weaver (eds), *International Political Economy: Debating the Past, Present and Future*, London: Routledge, pp. 169–177.

Kuhn, Thomas S. (1962), *The Structure of Scientific Revolutions*, Chicago, IL: University of Chicago Press.

Leander, Anna (2009), "Why we need multiple stories about the global political economy," *Review of International Political Economy*, **16** (2), 321–328.

McNamara, Kathleen (2011), "Of intellectual monocultures and the study of IPE," in Nicola Phillips and Catherine E. Weaver (eds), *International Political Economy: Debating the Past, Present and Future*, London: Routledge, pp. 64–73.

Payne, Anthony (2005), "The study of governance in a global political economy," in Nicola Phillips (ed.), *Globalizing International Political Economy*, New York: Palgrave Macmillan, pp. 55–81.

Porter, Tony (2001), "Can there be national perspectives on inter(national) relations?," in Robert M.A. Crawford and Darryl S.L. Jarvis (eds), *International Relations – Still an American Social Science? Toward Diversity in International Thought*, Albany, NY: State University of New York Press, pp. 131–147.

Ravenhill, John (2008), "In search of the missing middle," *Review of International Political Economy*, **15** (1), 18–29.

Schumpeter, Joseph (1942), *Capitalism, Socialism, and Democracy*, New York: Harper and Brothers.

Strange, Susan (1970), "International economics and international relations: a case of mutual neglect," *International Affairs*, **46** (2), 304–315.

Underhill, Geoffrey R.D. (2000), "State, market, and global political economy: genealogy of an (inter-?) discipline," *International Affairs*, **76** (4), 805–824.

Viner, Jacob (1948), "Power and plenty as objectives of foreign policy in the seventeenth and eighteenth centuries," *World Politics*, **1** (1), 1–29.

Wæver, Ole (1998), "The sociology of a not so international discipline: American and European developments in international relations," *International Organization*, **52** (4), 687–727.

Watson, Matthew (2005), *Foundations of International Political Economy*, New York: Palgrave Macmillan.

Watson, Matthew (2011), "The historical roots of theoretical traditions in global political economy," in John Ravenhill (ed.), *Global Political Economy*, New York: Oxford University Press, pp. 29–66.

2 The American school

We begin with the American school, considered by many to be the reigning version of IPE. Nowhere in the world are there more scholars claiming a specialty in the field than in the United States. Though numbers are hard to come by, a recent study suggests that as much as half of the global IPE community is located within America's borders (Sharman and Weaver 2013), and most of those can be assumed to be not too far from the prevailing mainstream. No other version of IPE is more widely disseminated. For some, the American school sets the standard by which all other factions may be judged. Many measure the value of their own contributions by comparison with the content or style of the school.

From the start, IPE in the United States has been mainly seen as a sub-specialty of the study of IR – in effect, a branch of political science. On occasion a few economists have chosen to enter the field, but not often. I myself have been described as "one of the rare cases of an economist who came in from the cold" (Underhill 2000: 811). For the most part, the terrain has been left to political scientists, and it is they who have put their stamp on how IPE is thought about in most of US academia – what we may call the mainstream American style.

Foremost this means that IPE in America is, above all, about sovereign states. As in IR more generally, the state is seen as the fundamental locus of authority. No other actor enjoys the legitimacy that comes with internationally recognized sovereignty, nor can any other actor legally exercise the ultimate right of coercion. Ontology, therefore, is narrowly state-centric. In the words of one popular textbook, IPE "is concerned with the interaction between the state, a sovereign territorial unit, and the market" (Cohn 2012: 3). Or as a prominent American scholar puts it: "The central questions all relate to the interaction of politics and economics among states" (Milner 2002: 214). National governments are the core actors. State policy-making is the main concern.

Further, most scholarship in the United States tends to hew closely to the norms of conventional US social science. Priority is given to scientific method – what may be called a pure or hard science model. Analysis is based on the twin principles of positivism and empiricism, which hold that knowledge is best accumulated through an appeal to objective observation and the systematic evaluation of evidence using rigorous quantitative or qualitative methodologies. Grand conceptualization is generally eschewed. Instead, most emphasis is placed on mid-level theory concentrating on key relationships isolated within a broader structure whose characteristics are unquestioned and assumed, normally, to be stable.

The purpose of analysis in the American school is to explain and understand how the world works, not to judge it. Normative concerns, for the most part, are downplayed. Serious scholarship is not to be sullied by personal values or policy advocacy. Theoretical inspiration is drawn largely from two disciplines – modern IPE's twin ancestors, economics and political science. Ideas or insights from other scholarly specialties rarely draw much systematic attention. Analysis tends to concentrate on two major sets of issues. One is the question of state behavior. How do we understand the policies of national governments in the global economy? The other is the question of system governance. How do states cope with the consequences of economic interdependence? These two issues constitute what, in formal language, may be called the American school's core "problematique."

State behavior

First on the agenda is state behavior. What motivates government policy, and how are policy preferences best explained and evaluated? Drawing on broader IR theory, these questions have come to be seen as a matter of "levels of analysis." More recently, the mutilevel approach has been codified by the eminent scholar David Lake (2006, 2009, 2011) under the rubric of Open Economy Politics (OEP).

Levels of analysis

For the American school, understanding state behavior is the central imperative. However, that does not mean the traditional billiard-ball model of rational, unitary actors conceived as closed black boxes driven solely by calculations of national interest and power. It is important not to mistake the meaning of state-centrism. For US scholars, state-centrism simply means privileging the state above other units of interest. It does not mean ignoring other actors. Many other agents may figure prominently in analysis – ranging from individuals and enterprises to multilateral organizations and transnational communities – but mainly for whatever role they play as influences or constraints on government policy. The state is prioritized.

In principle, three broad levels of analysis are distinguished, each a general theoretical orientation corresponding to one of the well-known "images" of international relations initially sketched by the well-known IR theorist Kenneth Waltz. In his classic *Man, the State, and War* (1959), Waltz sought to categorize the causes of war in as concise a fashion as possible. Any possible *casus belli*, he suggested could usefully be ordered under one of three headings: (1) within individuals; (2) within individual states; or (3) within the structure of the inter-state system. The first of his three images stressed defects in human nature; the second stressed defects in the internal organization of states; and the third stressed defects in states' external organization (the anarchic inter-state system). Today these are referred to, respectively, as the first, second, and third images of international relations.

Corresponding to Waltz's third image is the familiar *systemic* (or structural) level of analysis, which like so much of IR theory focuses on the sovereign state itself, promoting or defending its national interest in an insecure world. The methodological value of this type of approach is that it makes government preferences constants (exogenous) rather than covariates (endogenous) for purposes of analysis. Conceptions of national interest are assumed to be given and unchanging. Inquiry thus may concentrate exclusively on constraints and incentives for policy deriving from the broader structure of inter-state relations. Behavior, as Waltz later put it, may be studied from the "outside-in" (Waltz 1979: 63).

Conversely, in the tradition of comparative politics, behavior can also be studied from the "inside-out," concentrating on the internal characteristics of states rather than their external environment. That is the object of the so-called *domestic* level of analysis in IR, corresponding to Waltz's second image. Attention is directed to the strategic interactions among all domestic actors, inside or outside government, with actual or potential influence on a state's foreign actions, as well as to the institutional settings through which diverse interests are mediated and converted into policy – in short, the political and institutional basis at home for policy preferences abroad.

Finally, there is the *cognitive* level of analysis, analogous to Waltz's first image, which focuses on the base of ideas and consensual knowledge that lend legitimacy to governmental policy-making – an approach that contrasts sharply with the rational-actor models characteristic of the systemic and domestic levels of analysis. As initially conceived, the cognitive level was largely based in psychology and, following Waltz, concerned strictly with the mentality of the individual. What is in a person's mind? What is the independent influence of personal values and beliefs? In addition, in more recent years, the cognitive approach has also spawned a second track under the newly fashionable label of constructivism. In contrast to the political psychology track, the constructivist track is more sociological in nature, concerned with connections between individuals – with learning, inter-subjectivity, and social knowledge. How do meanings come to be attached to raw reality, and how do these "social facts" change over time? The spotlight of constructivism is on the independent effect of norms on state behavior. The two tracks are obviously complementary.

In practice, most attention in the American school is directed toward the systemic and domestic levels of analysis and the interaction between them. As two leading US scholars put it in an authoritative survey: "The most challenging questions in IPE have to do with the interaction of domestic and international factors as they affect economic policies and outcomes . . . [We] need to take into account both the domestic political economy of foreign economic policy and the role of strategic interaction among nation-states" (Frieden and Martin 2002: 119–120). The field's cutting edge, they say, is the "international-domestic research frontier." Lake, adopting the term Open Economy Politics from comparativist Robert Bates (1997), describes the synthesis of second- and third-image analysis as the "dominant approach [that] now structures and guides research" (Lake 2006: 757). For the American school, the international-domestic frontier is where the action is.

Open Economy Politics

Open Economy Politics, as Lake summarizes it, is largely rationalist in orientation and builds outward in linear fashion from the interests of individuals and other social units at the domestic level to the policy preferences of states and strategic interactions at the international level. For analytical purposes, the paradigm is decomposed into three distinct steps.

First come groups of individuals – for example, enterprises, sectors, or factors of production – that can reasonably be assumed to share more or less the same interests. Defined as preferences over alternative outcomes, interests are derived from established economic theories highlighting the distributional implications of different national policies. Attitudes toward the issue of import protection, for instance, are inferred from standard international trade models such as the familiar factor-endowments (Heckscher–Ohlin) theory. In turn, much depends on how units are located relative to others in the international economy. Constituencies more exposed to external market forces, for example, can be expected to have preferences that differ systematically from more insular sectors or industries. Significant contributions along these lines include work by Jeffry Frieden (1991) on financial interests and by Michael Hiscox (2002) on preferences over trade policy.

Next, OEP turns to how interests are aggregated and mediated through domestic political institutions. Drawing on familiar models from political science, the approach theorizes how divergent interests may be translated through political processes into public policy. Will outcomes differ in autocracies and democracies? In representative political regimes, how might outcomes be affected by electoral rules or partisan politics? Does the number of veto players matter? Institutions condition the nature of bargaining between groups – for example, by defining possible side-payments, cross-issue linkages, or log rolls. State preferences thus are assumed to be driven from the inside-out rather than the outside-in. The acknowledged "father"of the approach is Peter Katzenstein (1976), who very early stressed the role of domestic "structures" as an explanation of state behavior in IPE. A memorable example of the inside-out approach is provided by Beth Simmons (1994) in her classic study of the period between the two world wars, *Who Adjusts?*, which focuses attention squarely on the domestic sources of foreign economic policy.

Finally, once policy preferences are determined, OEP assumes a stage of international bargaining as states seek to influence one another's behavior, either explicitly or implicitly. Here, as John Odell (2000) has deftly shown, conventional negotiation models can play a role, emphasizing a myriad of considerations such as relative and absolute costs, time horizons, and each government's ability to make credible threats or promises. At issue are the distributional consequences of alternative joint outcomes. Each state is naturally assumed to seek the best possible deal it can.

In academic journals and books alike, US scholars have applied the OEP paradigm to virtually every issue area in the world economy – trade policy, monetary and financial relations, foreign direct investment, migration, foreign aid, natural resources, and environmental policy, to name just the most obvious. In formal terms, the "scope" of analysis (the range of issues addressed) is broad. Geographic coverage (formally, the "domain" of analysis) has also been broad, addressing policy behavior in every continent and region. Collectively, within its state-centric ontology, the American school's agenda knows few bounds, although, not surprisingly, the perspective of the United States is usually very much in mind. Implicit if not explicit in much research is the question of what it all means for the United States or its leadership role in the world.

Individual contributions, however, are typically more modest – what might be described as "small-bore" or mid-level in ambition – focusing on just bits of the picture rather than the whole. Formally, all three steps of the OEP paradigm – interests, institutions, and international bargaining – are needed to provide a comprehensive explanation of state behavior. As a practical matter, however, most scholars prefer to concentrate on just one or two of the steps, treating the remainder as exogenous in order to concentrate on a smaller and more tractable set of causal relations. Analysis is partial-equilibrium (holding many variables constant) rather than general-equilibrium in nature. Some discussions assume that interests are given in order to study how different domestic institutions aggregate or refract preferences under varying circumstances. Others set aside the complexities of domestic politics in order to isolate the direct impact of constituency preferences on policy. Yet others may simply assume a set of policy interests in order to evaluate the dynamics of international bargaining. In principle, nothing stands in the way of a more general-equilibrium approach that would bind the components together into a more complete whole. A valiant attempt along these lines was made a few years ago by the noted scholar Helen Milner (1997), seeking to combine the domestic and international levels of analysis in a grand theoretical approach. However, as Lake (2009: 225) ruefully acknowledges, "in practice synthesis remains imperfect." Theorizing, for the most part, remains determinedly mid-level.

System governance

The other half of the agenda is system governance. How do governments manage their mutual relations? Again drawing on broader IR theory, the question is addressed as a collective action problem. The challenge is to sustain cooperation or avoid conflict among states. The goal is to preserve the benefits of a healthy world economy.

The essence of governance lies in the authority to define and enforce norms for the allocation of values in a collectivity – to write the rules of the game, as it were. In the international system, however, where sovereignty stops at the national frontier, no such authority exists, at least not in formal terms. There is no recognized form of government at the global level. Rather, we live in a world of "governance without government" – a patchwork universe of imperfect substitutes for the real thing. That is especially evident in the realm of economic affairs, where distributional issues are persistently contested. In one guise or another, bargaining among states over their economic policies goes on all the time. The challenge of system governance is the third step of the OEP paradigm writ large.

So who is in charge? Back when the American school was still in its infancy, much attention was paid to so-called hegemonic stability theory (HST) – the idea that a stable global economy required one dominant leader, a hegemon, willing and able to use its preponderance of power to promote common objectives. For US scholars, obviously cognizant of their own country's outsized place in the world, a preoccupation with power seemed only natural – especially at a time when the capabilities of the United States, it appeared, might actually be in decline. In time, however, the weaknesses of HST became evident, as analysis demonstrated that hegemony could be considered neither necessary nor sufficient to sustain economic stability (Lake 1993). HST played an important role in reminding everyone of the political underpinnings of global economic governance. However, a narrow preoccupation with hegemony itself, it became clear, was really beside the point. The real issue was not a concentration of power. Rather, it had to do with the conditions that facilitate successful collective action by some or all of the community of nations.

Accordingly, the focus of analysis eventually shifted, first to the newfangled notion of international regimes and then, starting in the 1990s, to the broader role of international institutions. Regimes, in a famous collection of essays published in 1983 under the title *International Regimes* (Krasner 1983), were defined as "sets of implicit or explicit principles, norms, rules, and decision-making procedures around which actors' expectation converge in a given area of international relations." Later, regime analysis was folded into a more general study of international institutions, conceived as "persistent and connected sets of rules (formal and informal) that prescribe behavioral roles, constrain activity, and shape expectations" (Keohane 1989: 3). International institutions, which may or may not be embodied in tangible organizations, can be understood to encompass all forms of patterned cooperation among states. As such, they serve to aggregate preferences into policy; when preferences clash, they provide a mechanism for conflict resolution. They are, in short, the glue that holds the system together.

In practical terms, international institutions play multiple roles. Like their domestic counterparts, they affect outcomes by structuring the process of implicit or explicit bargaining among actors. Absent world government, they can facilitate inter-state cooperation by providing information, articulating norms, or offering convenient venues for the resolution of conflicts. Insofar as they establish verifiable standards, they make it easier for governments to evaluate one another's intentions. Likewise, by defining "focal points" on which all parties can agree, they help to resolve distributional disputes that might otherwise impede cooperation. To the extent that they afford participants the opportunity to adjust commitments in light of changing circumstances, governments will be less tempted to abandon obligations that happen to become inconvenient.

Today, institutional theory is at the center of the American school's study of system governance. While some scholars focus on issues of compliance – why and how states obey international rules – others concentrate on how institutions might best be structured to achieve desired outcomes. A representative collection of essays is provided by Lisa Martin and Beth Simmons (2001). Another notable volume, edited by Judith Goldstein and colleagues (Goldstein *et al.* 2001), addresses the role that legalization can play in raising the cost of exit from prior commitments; a third, edited by Barbara Koremenos and associates (Koremenos *et al.* 2003), explores issues of optimal institutional design. Here too, analysis tends to be broad in both scope and domain, encompassing virtually every issue in the world economy, from trade and money to migration and the environment, as well as extending to every corner of the globe. Again, within its state-centric ontology, the American school's agenda knows few bounds.

Debates

After more than four decades of growth, the American school has clearly come to dominate discourse among scholars in the United States. In top rated journals such as *International Organization* or *International Studies Quarterly*, the influence of the OEP paradigm is pervasive. The pattern has been confirmed by successive surveys of the field of international relations conducted by researchers at the College of William and Mary in Williamsburg, Virginia – the so-called Teaching, Research, and International Policy (TRIP) Project, based on both opinion polls and a review of a dozen journals in the IR field. The latest TRIP survey, undertaken in 2011 and covering teaching, research, and policy views of faculty in 20 countries, was published in 2012 (Maliniak *et al.* 2012). Earlier surveys took place in 2004, 2006, and 2008. After I first spoke of a transatlantic divide, two of the researchers responsible for the project, reviewing their accumulated data, concluded that "the picture that Cohen paints of an American school of IPE is largely consistent with our findings" (Maliniak and Tierney 2011: 30).

Likewise, the style predominates in key institutional settings, such as the Political Economy Section of the American Political Science Association (APSA) and the International Political Economy Section of the International Studies Association (ISA). Little else can be found in the papers presented at the annual meetings of the International Political Economy Society (IPES), a new association created in 2007 that has quickly become the premiere venue for current IPE scholarship in the United States. It is no accident that the founding father of IPES was none other than David Lake.

The school's dominance is not absolute, of course. A look beyond the small number of top-ranked journals covered by the TRIP surveys to other more specialized journals and to book publishing reveals considerably more diversity in US IPE scholarship (Sharman and Weaver 2013). In the words of one astute observer (Germain 2011: 97–98), the TRIP data represent only "a narrow slice of IPE that cannot be considered to be the field as a whole ... a pinched portrayal of IPE in America." A more expansive picture would include other slices as well, representing what Ravenhill (2008) has called the "missing middle." Included would be any number of familiar names – among many others, Daniel Drezner (2007), an authority on international governance issues; Jonathan Kirshner (1995, 2007), who has written extensively on money and power; Kathleen McNamara (1998), an early exponent of cognitive analysis in IPE; Dani Rodrik (2011), an expert on the politics of globalization; and Herman Schwartz (2010), who has carefully analyzed state-market relations in historical context. The "missing middle" too is part of IPE in America.

However, as students of the subject quickly learn, there is also a high degree of hierarchy in US IPE. Writing about the American study of international relations, political scientist Thomas Biersteker (2009: 310–311) notes that "within the US there is hegemony of a relatively small number of leading research departments and universities . . . disciplining and defining the field of study . . . what they consider to be 'good' social science." Along similar lines, Wæver (1998: 726) speaks of "an apex that . . . comes to serve as the global core of the discipline." Much the same can be said of the American study of IPE. A relatively small number of prestigious institutions and publishing venues have an outsized effect on what aspiring academics know they must do to land a good job, win research funding, or get on the program at major professional meetings. The TRIP data may not capture the full *breadth* of the field as it actually exists in the United States, but the surveys arguably do succeed in highlighting what is done at the *peak* of the field, where standards are established and ambitions are defined. The dozen journals reviewed in the project are selected on the basis of their "impact" as measured by numbers of citations; as the top-ranked journals, their influence is bound to be widespread. Even among those whose professional preferences might differ, there is a high degree of consensus on what these journals have to say about the basic norms of the field – what is or is not to be considered "good" scholarship. The greatest respect goes to those whose work is in the highly demanding style of the American school.

None of this, however, is meant to suggest that the mainstream American school marches in monolithic, lock-step uniformity. Beyond the fundamentals of paradigm and agenda, the faction does not lack within-type variance. Scholars largely agree on the need for a state-centric ontology; they concur as well on what constitutes the fundamental problematique for analysis. Yet there is also much disagreement on more specific questions, reflecting broad debates that have gone on among IR theorists for years. In practice, the American school of IPE encompasses a multiplicity of traditions that can all claim a degree of intellectual legitimacy (Cohen 2009b).

Recall the three "models of the future" – liberalism, Marxism, and realism – as outlined by Robert Gilpin back in the field's early years. Marxism, for the most part, was quickly relegated to the sidelines (though by no means forgotten, as we shall see in the next chapter). However, variants of realism and liberalism soon engaged in a duel for influence that has lasted for decades. At issue is the nature of the underlying connection between economic and political activity, an age-old question that has long divided scholars of political economy. Does economics drive politics, or vice versa? Central to liberalism (later, neoliberal institutionalism) is a belief that economics dominates politics – meaning, in particular, the forces of market competition and incentives for material advancement. Realism (later neorealism), by contrast, has always retained faith in the capacity of political factors – especially the distribution of power among states – to shape economic systems. Correspondingly, realists have always favored the systemic level of analysis, where power and politics are central. Liberals, on the other hand, are more comfortable with the domestic level of analysis, where economic relations mold the constellations of interest that are assumed to be at the heart of the policy process.

Perhaps most illustrative of the divide is the prolonged debate over the issue of intergovernmental cooperation on major economic issues: the challenge of governance. For liberals like Robert Keohane – perhaps the best known of the early pioneers of IPE in the United States – the prospect of mutual gain should suffice to encourage states to make the compromises needed to achieve effective collective action. That was the premise underlying Keohane's so-called functional-ist approach to the problem, stressing a demand for institutionalized cooperation derived from anticipated benefits (Keohane 1983, 1984). For realists, by contrast, prospects for successful collective action appear much dimmer because of a presumed preoccupation with distributional issues. States in an anarchic world are thought to be concerned more with relative than absolute gains. As Joseph Grieco (1988) wrote in a classic article, governments can be expected to act like "defensive positionalists," resisting agreements that promise more benefit to potential adversaries than to themselves.

In time, the differences between liberalism and realism have come to seem less crucial than their similarities – in particular, their effective convergence around what John Ruggie (1999: 215) has called "neo-utilitarian precepts and premises." Both traditions shared a preference for a rationalist and materialist approach to analysis. Actors, whether states or nonstate entities, are assumed to act in pursuit of clearly defined interests, usually expressed in terms of material preferences and goals. Identities are well established and unchanging. Outcomes are the result of a careful balancing of costs and benefits of alternative paths of behavior.

Instead, the most vigorous debates today are between neo-utilitarianism of any kind, on the one hand, and cognitive analysis on the other, whether based in personal psychology or sociological connections. Leading the way on the psychological track is Odell (2000), whose explorations of the bargaining process among states highlights the role of negotiators' beliefs as an independent influence on strategies and outcomes. The critical issue, he suggests, is what Nobel prize-winning economist Herbert Simon called "bounded rationality" – a variant of "rational choice that takes into account the cognitive limitations of the decision maker, limitations of both knowledge and computational capacity" (Simon 1997: 291). Given the constraints of bounded rationality, negotiators typically make use of cognitive shortcuts, convenient heuristics that rely heavily on subjective beliefs to guide their actions. To understand economic diplomacy, therefore, it is vital to understand the ideas of the diplomats. More recent work along these lines has borrowed from the newly fashionable branch of economics known as behavioral economics, which demonstrates how such concepts as framing, loss aversion, fairness, and myopic time horizons help to explain state behavior (Elms 2006; Kapstein 2008).

Systematic constructivist-style research has also begun to emerge on the sociological track – especially, as it happens, involving monetary or financial matters where issues of reputation and perception are obviously critical. A prime example comes from Jeffrey Chwieroth (2010) in a study of the International Monetary Fund and the rise of financial liberalization in emerging market economies in the 1980s and 1990s. Capital markets were opened, Chwieroth contends, because of a new set of neoliberal norms that were diffused through a network of knowledge-based experts once they came to positions of political authority at the Fund and in national governments. The spread of constructivism among younger members of the American school of IPE, posing a direct challenge to the dominance of more traditional neo-utilitarian approaches, is well documented in a recent collection of essays edited by Rawi Abdelal and colleagues (Abdelal *et al.* 2010).

Hard science

On one point, however, there is scarcely any debate: methodology. It matters little whether analysis is directed toward some aspect of state behavior or to the challenge of system governance. Nor does it matter whether scholars are more inclined toward a neo-utilitarian or a cognitive view of the world. Whatever the agenda or theoretical disposition, the preferred epistemology is the same: a hard science model based on the twin principles of positivism and empiricism. Above all, the American school prizes objective observation and the systematic evaluation of evidence. Conjectures in some form are specified, based on deductive reasoning, and then tested for accuracy – a process known formally as "hypothetico-deductivism." In the words of Stephen Krasner, another of the American school's earliest stars: "International political economy is deeply embedded in the standard methodology of the social sciences which, stripped to its bare bones, simply means stating a proposition and testing it against external evidence" (Krasner 1996: 108–109).

It was not always this way. Among the pioneers of the field in the United States, back in the 1970s and 1980s – including in particular Keohane, Gilpin, Katzenstein, and Krasner – more informal methods predominated. In my earlier *Intellectual History*, I referred to these extraordinary thinkers as the First Generation of IPE in the United States. Relying mainly on qualitative analysis, Keohane and his colleague Joseph Nye (Keohane and Nye 1977) taught us to think intuitively in terms of a world economy characterized by multiple channels of communications, an absence of hierarchy among issues, and a diminished role for military force – what they called "complex interdependence" – while Gilpin, with his three "models," helped us to organize our theorizing for ready comparison and contrast. The role of hegemony and leadership was highlighted by Gilpin and Krasner; the role of international institutions, by Krasner and Keohane; and the role of second-image, and later, first-image analysis, by Katzenstein.

However, soon epistemological standards began to tighten, beginning with a Second Generation that came to maturity in the 1980s and 1990s determined to build on the foundations laid by the early pioneers. Important new insights on trade issues were provided by the likes of Judith Goldstein and Helen Milner, adding considerably to our understanding of factors affecting both state policies and system governance. On financial issues key contributions came from, among others, Jeffry Frieden and Miles Kahler. Joanne Gowa and David Lake helped to clarify questions posed by the prolonged debate over hegemonic stability theory. Lisa Martin and Beth Simmons broadened the scope of institutional theory, and John Odell and John Ruggie made early efforts to bring cognitive analysis into the field.

Then, starting in the last decade of the twentieth century, came a Third Generation that tilted even more in the direction of a hard science model – featuring increasingly well-known names like Lawrence Broz, Jeffrey Chwieroth, Michael Hiscox, David Leblang, Layna Mosley, and Michael Tomz. Second Generation scholars did not entirely eschew formal modeling or systematic empirical analysis, but neither were these elements central to their research efforts. Among Third Generation scholars, by contrast, hypothetico-deductivism has taken over as the American school's dominant methodology – the truest measure of scholarship. The trend is readily apparent in the successive TRIP surveys, which reveal a glaring generation gap among US respondents who listed IPE as their primary or secondary area of research. Of those polled in the 2006 survey who received their doctorates in the 1980s, only 18 percent identified quantitative methods as their primary approach. By contrast, the share jumped to 27 percent for those who completed their degrees in the 1990s, and to 36 percent for those finishing their studies in 2000 or later (Maliniak and Tierney 2011: 25).

Today, for many, the Third Generation's increasingly strict adherence to scientific method has become the defining characteristic of US IPE – the real divide between the American school and others. As the Canadian Eric Helleiner (2011: 179, 183) observes, "If a sharp division has emerged in the field, then it has come more recently . . . The more serious division that has emerged is between the Third Generation of the American school and everyone else (including many in the US school who remain inspired by its pioneers' vision of the field)." Those in the "missing middle" are often treated as outsiders, not part of the inner circle.

For the most part, the American school's methodological approach is borrowed from neoclassical economics, which in turn got it from the physical sciences. Neoclassical is the label given to the mainstream discipline of economics following the profession's divorce from political science in the late nineteenth century. Since then, economic scholarship has grown increasingly abstract, relying ever more on deductive logic and parsimonious models to pare messy reality down to its bare essentials. The prevailing style, as in the physical sciences, is reductionist. The aim is to uncover universal truths – "to predict something large from something small," as a prominent economist once put it (Johnson 1971: 9). Since its infancy, the modern field of IPE in the United States has come to aspire to that same degree of strict numeracy and parsimony, in effect mimicking the economics profession. In my *Intellectual History* I referred to this trend as a kind of "creeping economism." In the search for empirical regularities, research methods have become increasingly standardized, stressing above all formal propositions and rigorous testing. The emphasis is on technical sophistication and intellectual elegance.

Most prized are purely quantitative methods based on large sets of detailed statistical data – for example, regression analysis or large-scale survey research. However, respectability is accorded even to more qualitative approaches, such as structured case studies, textual analysis, or social experiments, so long as they appear to meet strict scientific standards. The aim is to promote a cumulation of knowledge through replicable tests of falsifiable hypotheses. The hope is to achieve results that hold up under a wide variety of circumstances ("external validity"). The goal, ultimately, is to attain a greater understanding of the world in which we live, untainted by subjectivity or prejudice.

Many reasons have been suggested for the American school's love affair with scientific method – editorial control of journals, the standards applied in tenure or promotion cases, the way graduate students are taught. However, these are more symptom than cause. Underlying all the school's practices of intellectual reproduction is a deeper issue, involving political scientists and their peers in the economics profession. To be blunt, political scientists in the United States have an inferiority complex when it comes to economics – what I have elsewhere described as a case of "peer-us envy" (Cohen 2009a). Even some of the top names in mainstream IPE bow their heads, describing neoclassical economics as "the reigning king of the social sciences" (Katzenstein *et al.* 1999: 23). Whether the title is deserved or not, it is certainly true that the reductionist style of economics has come to set the standard for what passes for professionalism among US social scientists. If today the most highly rated work in American IPE tends to mimic the economist's demanding hard science model, it is largely to demonstrate that political scientists, for all the ambiguities of the political process, are no less capable of precise and formal rigor. Specialists in IPE want respect too.

A maturing interdiscipline?

Not surprisingly, American school scholars express much pride in the way their version of the field has developed. The triumph of OEP, backed by hard science research methods, is seen as a mark of genuine intellectual progress – in Lake's words, a true maturing of what he calls the "interdiscipline" of IPE (Lake 2006). In his words: "This young field is rapidly maturing. From a range of early perspectives, a dominant approach referred to as Open Economy Politics (OEP), now structures and guides research . . . IPE is now centered on, if you will, a hegemonic approach" (Lake 2006: 757, 772). In effect – to appropriate the language of Thomas Kuhn (1962) – a "paradigm shift" has occurred, leading to a new era of "normal science." Again in Lake's words, "By the mid-1990s, OEP had dramatically reshaped the study of IPE in the United States and stimulated an ongoing period of Kuhnian normalcy" (Lake 2011: 47).

Such pride is by no means misplaced. As a group, US political scientists deserve credit for genuinely seeking to bridge the void between international economics and IR, in the spirit of Strange's 1970 manifesto. Many have gone to great pains to learn at least the rudiments of economic theory and methodology. Economists, sadly, with few exceptions, have failed to return the compliment, remaining largely deaf to the politics of international economic relations.

Moreover, the prevailing US style of IPE does offer notable advantages. Indeed, the value added is unmistakable. On the one hand, a firm theoretical foundation is provided at all three stages of the OEP paradigm. Rather than simply introducing preferences by assumption or by inferring them from observed behavior (a form of circular reasoning), interests are derived from prior, robust economic theory. Likewise, established political models are used to undergird analysis of the role of institutions and bargaining at both the domestic and international levels. From start to finish, therefore, theorizing is explicit. That not only places discussion on a sound deductive footing. It also enlarges the scope of scholarship, providing tools to address a wide range of practical issues. At the same time, a firm empirical basis is assured by the priority given to systematic testing of evidence. The hard science model offers both rigor and replicability, thus promoting a broad cumulation of knowledge. Imprecision, to the extent possible, is banished from discourse.

Yet the style also has distinct limits, despite its popularity. In ontological terms, the American school can be faulted for its strict state-centrism, which discounts the importance of other units of analysis, from the individual to the global. Michael Zürn, a noted German political scientist, speaks of the "analytical shackles of 'methodological nationalism'" (Zürn 2013: 416) – the restraints of a narrow focus on national governments, which automatically excludes alternative ways of thinking about the world. Admittedly, even in an era of globalization, the sovereign state remains a key actor – but it is not always the key actor. Others may matter in their own right, not just for whatever role they play as influences or constraints on government policy. Many observers would question why the state must necessarily be prioritized for purposes of analysis.

Worse, even within the school's state-centric approach, much seems to be missing. As already noted, synthesis of the three stages of the OEP paradigm remains imperfect at best. Grand conceptualization, integrating the separate levels of analysis, is generally avoided. Instead, most in the American school seem content to stick to theorizing at the mid-level, where broader structures are simply taken for granted. The Big Picture gets ignored, if not forgotten.

Why is the Big Picture ignored? In good part, the omission seems to be due to the inherent limitations of a reductionist approach to scholarship, which naturally diverts attention from the big to the small. It is surely easier to focus research in high definition if many variables can be assumed to be exogenous. If the challenge is to formulate parsimonious models and clearly falsifiable hypotheses, it is more convenient to disaggregate inquiry in order to make it analytically tractable. The more fine-grained the analysis, the greater is the ability to derive precise causal theorems. The appeal of a search for universal truths is seductive.

However, seduction can also be risky, as we know. The preference for partial-equilibrium analysis rests on an untested assumption that the

Big Picture simply does not matter. All that counts are the domestic determinants of foreign economic policy, which can safely be treated as exogenous. In effect, the reductionist style places a bet that larger influences that may inhere in the system as a whole play no role in determining outcomes; no linkages or feedbacks from broader macro-processes need be considered. Thomas Oatley (2011) calls this the "reductionist gamble." As Oatley points out, to the extent that causal forces may in fact originate outside of domestic politics, OEP analysis will almost certainly draw inaccurate inferences.

Why, then, does reductionism remain the American school's preferred style? Above all, the popularity of the approach seems to be attributable to the pragmatic requirements of empiricism, which tend to shrink scholarly ambitions. By definition, a hard science model depends on the availability of reliable data. Research, accordingly, tends to become data-driven, diverted away from issues that lack the requisite base of information. In effect, scientific method plays a key role in defining *what* will be studied, automatically marginalizing grander questions that cannot be reduced to a manageable set of regressions or structured case-study analysis.

Defenders of normal science would object, arguing that without some form of empirical verification it is impossible to judge the value of new notions or insights. Hypothetico-deductivism is essential. Yet that line of defense is porous at best, underestimating the usefulness of pure theorizing or sketchy speculation as a stimulus to thinking outside the box. How many times in the past has a seminal idea begun with little or no data to support it? In international economics, Nobel-laureate Robert Mundell invented a whole new branch of study, optimum currency area theory, with a brief article that included not a single shred of hard evidence (Mundell 1961). In IPE, two decades of rich debate over hegemonic stability theory were stimulated by the early writings of Robert Gilpin based on the flimsiest of historical analogies (Gilpin 1975). To insist that from the start every theory must be backed with hard evidence is to risk discouraging truly innovative scholarship.

In practice, it is clear that the American style of IPE does not come without cost. As Keohane (2011: 38) lamented recently, commenting on the creeping economism of the field he was so instrumental in starting, "a price has been paid." One cost is a loss of descriptive reality or credibility. The full flavor of life is sacrificed for what a critic calls a "tasteless pottage of mathematical models" (DeLong 2005: 128), often wholly unintelligible to a wider public. Instead, the true character of life may be caricatured by the often implausible assumptions that parsimony demands. Analysis is increasingly detached from real-world institutions and events, becoming more a branch of applied mathematics than a true *social* science. An even greater cost is a failure to address many important issues – particularly questions involving underlying structures or broad changes in the global political economy. In the American school, big systemic questions are most conspicuous by their absence. Holistic thinking about the system as a whole is rare.

Consider, for example, the great financial crisis that struck the world in 2008, threatening a new Great Depression. That calamity had all the earmarks of a genuine systemic transformation – the end of an era of widespread deregulation and expansion of financial markets. "The first crisis of the current era of globalization," one influential commentary called it, a shock that has "started to reshape the global economy and shift the balance between the political and economic forces at play" (Pisani-Ferry and Santos 2009: 8). Yet who in the American school even saw it coming? In retrospect, it is clear that there actually were a few US scholars who did seek to draw attention to some of the dangers lurking (Helleiner 2010). However, they were few and far between and scarcely heeded. For the most part, mainstream IPE in the United States simply ignored the possibility that such a massive shock could occur. The structure itself was not problematized. It was a grave case of myopia (Cohen 2009a).

In short, it may be true that the American school has matured into a stage of Kuhnian normalcy. The pride expressed by Lake and others is not unjustified. However, progress, it is clear, has been purchased at a high price, measured above all by how much gets left out. The school's omissions are as noteworthy as its accomplishments.

References

Abdelal, Rawi, Mark Blyth and Craig Parsons (eds) (2010), *Constructing the International Economy*, Ithaca, NY: Cornell University Press.

Bates, Robert (1997), *Open Economy Politics: The Political Economy of the World Coffee Trade*, Princeton, NJ: Princeton University Press.

Biersteker, Thomas J. (2009), "The parochialism of hegemony: challenges for 'American' international relations," in Arlene B. Tickner and Ole Wæver (eds), *International Relations Scholarship Around the World*, London: Routledge, pp. 308–327.

Chwieroth, Jeffrey (2010), *Capital Ideas: The IMF and the Rise of Financial Liberalization*, Princeton, NJ: Princeton University Press.

Cohen, Benjamin J. (2009a), "A grave case of myopia," *International Interactions*, **35** (4), 436–444.

Cohen, Benjamin J. (2009b), "The multiple traditions of American IPE," in Mark Blyth (ed.), *Routledge Handbook of International Political Economy (IPE): IPE as a Global Conversation*, London: Routledge, pp. 23–35.

Cohn, Theodore (2012), *Global Political Economy*, sixth edition, Boston: Longman.

DeLong, J. Bradford (2005), "Sisyphus as social democrat: the life and legacy of John Kenneth Galbraith," *Foreign Affairs*, **84** (3), 126–130.

Drezner, Daniel W. (2007), *All Politics is Global: Explaining International Regulatory Regimes*, Princeton, NJ: Princeton University Press.

Elms, Deborah Kay (2006), "New directions for IPE: drawing from behavioral economics," paper prepared for the inaugural meeting of the International Political Economy Society, Princeton, NJ, November.

Frieden, Jeffry A. (1991), "Invested interests: the politics of national economic policies in a world of global finance," *International Organization*, **45** (4), 425–451.

Frieden, Jeffry A. and Lisa L. Martin (2002), "International political economy: global and domestic interactions," in Ira Katznelson and Helen V. Milner (eds), *Political Science: State of the Discipline*, New York: Norton, pp. 118–146.

Germain, Randall D. (2011), "The 'American' school of IPE? A dissenting view," in Nicola Phillips and Catherine E. Weaver (eds), *International Political Economy: Debating the Past, Present and Future*, London: Routledge, pp. 83–91.

Gilpin, Robert (1975), *U.S. Power and the Multinational Corporation*, New York: Basic Books.

Goldstein, Judith L., Miles Kahler, Robert O. Keohane and Anne-Marie Slaughter (eds) (2001), *Legalization and World Politics*, Cambridge, MA: MIT Press.

Grieco, Joseph M. (1988), "Anarchy and the limits of cooperation: a realist critique of the newest liberal institutionalism," *International Organization*, **42** (3), 485–507.

Helleiner, Eric (2010), "Understanding the 2007–2008 global financial crisis: lessons for scholars of international political economy," *Annual Review of Political Science*, **14**, 67–87.

Helleiner, Eric (2011), "Division and dialogue in Anglo-American IPE: a reluctant Canadian view," in Nicola Phillips and Catherine E. Weaver (eds), *International Political Economy: Debating the Past, Present and Future*, London: Routledge, pp. 178–184.

Hiscox, Michael J. (2002), *International Trade and Political Conflict: Commerce, Coalitions, and Mobility*, Princeton, NJ: Princeton University Press.

Johnson, Harry G. (1971), "The Keynesian revolution and the monetarist counter-revolution," *American Economic Review*, **61** (2), 1–14.

Kapstein, Ethan (2008), "Fairness considerations in world politics: lessons from international trade negotiations," *Political Science Quarterly*, **123** (2), 229–246.

Katzenstein, Peter J. (1976), "International relations and domestic structures: foreign economic policies of advanced industrial states," *International Organization*, **30** (1), 1–45.

Katzenstein, Peter J., Robert O. Keohane and Stephen D. Krasner (1999), "*International Organization* and the study of world politics," in Peter J. Katzenstein, Robert O. Keohane and Stephen D. Krasner (eds), *Exploration and Contestation in the Study of World Politics*, Cambridge, MA: MIT Press, pp. 5–45.

Keohane, Robert O. (1983), "The demand for international regimes," in Stephen D. Krasner (ed.), *International Regimes*, Ithaca, NY: Cornell University Press, pp. 141–171.

Keohane, Robert O. (1984), *After Hegemony: Cooperation and Discord in the World Political Economy*, Princeton, NJ: Princeton University Press.

Keohane, Robert O. (1989), *International Institutions and State Power: Essays in International Relations Theory*, Boulder, CO: Westview Press.

Keohane, Robert O. (2011), "The old IPE and the new," in Nicola Phillips and Catherine E. Weaver (eds), *International Political Economy: Debating the Past, Present and Future*, London: Routledge, pp. 34–46.

Kirshner, Jonathan (1995), *Currency and Coercion: The Political Economy of International Monetary Power*, Princeton, NJ: Princeton University Press.

Kirshner, Jonathan (2007), *Appeasing Bankers: Financial Caution on the Road to War*, Princeton, NJ: Princeton University Press.

Koremenos, Barbara, Charles Lipson and Duncan Snidal (eds) (2003), *The Rational Design of International Institutions*, New York: Cambridge University Press.

Krasner, Stephen D. (ed.) (1983), *International Regimes*, Ithaca, NY: Cornell University Press.

Krasner, Stephen D. (1996), "The accomplishments of international political economy," in Steve Smith, Ken Booth and Marysia Zalewski (eds), *International Theory: Positivism and Beyond*, New York: Cambridge University Press, pp. 108–127.

Kuhn, Thomas S. (1962), *The Structure of Scientific Revolutions*, Chicago, IL: University of Chicago Press.

Lake, David A. (1993), "Leadership, hegemony, and the international economy: naked emperor or tattered monarch with potential?," *International Studies Quarterly*, **37** (4), 459–489.

Lake, David A. (2006), "International political economy: a maturing interdiscipline," in Barry R. Weingast and Donald A. Wittman (eds), *Oxford Handbook of Political Economy*, New York: Oxford University Press, pp. 757–777.

Lake, David A. (2009), "Open economy politics: a critical review," *Review of International Organizations*, **4** (3), 219–244.

Lake, David A. (2011), "TRIPs across the Atlantic: theory and epistemology in IPE," in Nicola Phillips and Catherine E. Weaver (eds), *International Political Economy: Debating the Past, Present and Future*, London: Routledge, pp. 45–52.

Maliniak, Daniel and Michael J. Tierney (2011), "The American school of IPE," in Nicola Phillips and Catherine E. Weaver (eds), *International Political Economy: Debating the Past, Present and Future*, London: Routledge, pp. 11–34.

Maliniak, Daniel, Susan Peterson and Michael J. Tierney (2012), *TRIP Around the World: Teaching, Research, and Policy Views of International Relations Faculty in 20 Countries*, Williamsburg, VA: College of William and Mary.

Martin, Lisa L. and Beth A. Simmons (eds) (2001), *International Institutions*, Cambridge, MA: MIT Press.

McNamara, Kathleen R. (1998), *The Currency of Ideas: Monetary Politics in the European Union*, Ithaca, NY: Cornell University Press.

Milner, Helen V. (1997), *Interests, Institutions, and Information: Domestic Politics and International Relations*, Princeton, NJ: Princeton University Press.

Milner, Helen V. (2002), "Reflections on the field of international political economy," in Michael Brecher and Frank P. Harvey (eds), *Conflict, Security, Foreign Policy, and International Political Economy: Past Paths and Future Directions in International Studies*, Ann Arbor, MI: University of Michigan Press, pp. 207–223.

Mundell, Robert A. (1961), "A theory of optimum currency areas," *American Economic Review*, **51** (4), 657–665.

Oatley, Thomas (2011), "The reductionist gamble: open economy politics in the global economy," *International Organization*, **65** (2), 311–341.

Odell, John S. (2000), *Negotiating the World Economy*, Ithaca, NY: Cornell University Press.

Pisani-Ferry, Jean and Indhira Santos (2009), "Reshaping the global economy," *Finance and Development*, **46** (1), 8–12.

Ravenhill, John (2008), "In search of the missing middle," *Review of International Political Economy*, **15** (1), 18–29.

Rodrik, Dani (2011), *The Globalization Paradox: Democracy and the Future of the World Economy*, New York: W.W. Norton.

Ruggie, John Gerard (1999), "What makes the world hang together? Neo-utilitarianism and the social constructivist challenge," in Peter J. Katzenstein, Robert O. Keohane and Stephen D. Krasner (eds), *Exploration and Contestation in the Study of World Politics*, Cambridge, MA: MIT Press, pp. 215–245.

Schwartz, Herman M. (2010), *States versus Markets: The Emergence of a Global Economy*, third edition, London: Palgrave Macmillan.

Sharman, Jason C. and Catherine Weaver (2013), "RIPE, the American school, and diversity in global IPE," *Review of International Political Economy*, **20** (5), in press.

Simmons, Beth A. (1994), *Who Adjusts? Domestic Sources of Foreign Economic Policy During the Interwar Years*, Princeton, NJ: Princeton University Press.

Simon, Herbert A. (1997), *Models of Bounded Rationality*, Volume 3: *Empirically Grounded Economic Reason*, Cambridge, MA: MIT Press.

Underhill, Geoffrey R.D. (2000), "State, market, and global political economy: genealogy of an (inter?) discipline," *International Affairs*, **76** (4), 805–824.

Wæver, Ole (1998), "The sociology of a not so international discipline: American and European developments in international relations," *International Organization*, **52** (4), 687–727.

Waltz, Kenneth N. (1959), *Man, the State, and War*, New York: Columbia University Press.

Waltz, Kenneth N. (1979), *Theory of International Politics*, Reading, MA: Addison-Wesley.

Zürn, Michael (2013), "Globalization and global governance," in Walter Carlsnaes, Thomas Risse and Beth A. Simmons (eds), *Handbook of International Relations*, second edition, London: Sage Publications, pp. 401–425.

3 America's "Left-Out"

In defining IPE as it is generally understood in the United States, the pre-eminence of the American school is undeniable. Yet the school is by no means the only show in town. Alternative conceptions of the field can also be found among US scholars, frequently labeled "heterodox" or "radical" to contrast with the prevailing orthodoxy. Although largely treated as outliers by mainstream theorists, these voices pose a challenge that cannot and should not be ignored. In a commentary on my *Intellectual History*, one esteemed heterodox scholar rightly took me to task for excluding more radical scholarship from consideration, which he wryly defined as "the 'Left-Out': scholars politically on the left" (Murphy 2011: 161). In fact, the Left-Out are an important part of the field and legitimately deserve our attention.

Central to the Left-Out is a rejection of the state-centric ontology of the American school. Priority, rather, is given more to the evolution of the global system as a whole, understood in terms of vast and complex historical structures. The core problematique is systemic transformation, with particular emphasis on transcendent issues of inequality, economic development, and social change. The purpose of research is normative, not just to explain things from a perch of high objectivity but to try to make the world a better place to live. Theoretical inspiration is drawn less from economics and political science and much more from a host of other related disciplines – not least, sociology. The hard science model of conventional social science is replaced by analysis that is more interpretative, even intuitive, in nature. Mid-level theory is considered timid. Grand conceptualization is not eschewed but celebrated.

Marxist roots

Although few of the Left-Out today would call themselves classical Marxists, the roots of Marxism are evident in much of their scholarship. For heterodox scholars in the United States, the analytical constructs and concerns of Marxist theory remain much more of an intellectual inspiration than either of Gilpin's other two "models of the future." That means, above all, a commitment to "historical materialism," which Karl Marx defined as "the materialist conception of history." The "materialism" in historical materialism means placing economic relations and the social organization of production at the very center of analysis. Here it is liberalism and realism that are largely relegated to the sidelines.

Marx and his disciples

Interestingly, Marx himself had remarkably little to say about the international dimension of political economy. He sought endlessly to expose the "laws of motion" of capitalist development. Yet in all his voluminous works, he rarely distinguished between the global and the domestic. His main focus was on the dynamics of capitalism as an integrated social system, dominated above all by what he saw as the central dilemma for capitalists: an inexorable tendency for the rate of profit to decline. The essence of the problem, as he saw it, was a core "internal contradiction" of the capitalist mode of production – a tendency for the physical stock of capital to grow too fast. Driven by the pressures of competition, capitalists invested too much, leading to an excess of production (overproduction) for which there were too few buyers (underconsumption). Could anything be done to cope with the contradiction? For Marx, there were several "countervailing forces" that could be used to sustain the rate of profit, at least for a time. Most obvious was the option to cut costs by suppressing wages, thus exploiting the working class. However, there were also other possibilities, including foreign trade. In one of his few allusions to the world economy, Marx specifically mentioned both access to cheap raw materials and the opportunity to sell profitably in overseas markets as potential countervailing strategies.

On this meager foundation, Marx's disciples eventually built a superstructure of theory purporting to explain much broader characteristics of the international system (Cohen 1973). Marx died in 1883, just as a new age of imperialism was dawning with what was to become a wild scramble by the world's richest countries for colonies in Africa and elsewhere. For Marx, it was too late to draw any connection between the so-called New Imperialism and capitalist dynamics. However, for many of those inspired by him, the link was soon obvious and in the decades to come became a cardinal article of faith. Imperialism was, as its base, an economic phenomenon.

For some Marxists, like the notorious revolutionary Rosa Luxemburg, the origins of economic imperialism lay in a lack of effective demand, owing to the inadequate purchasing power available to workers. The solution for capitalism lay in colonies that would provide needed additional markets. Yet for others, including most importantly V.I. Lenin, the link lay elsewhere, not in the commercial requirements of capitalism but in its *financial* requirements – the need for profitable outlets for surplus capital. Owing to pressures on the rate of profit at home, capitalists were driven to find new investment opportunities abroad. In *Imperialism, the Highest Stage of Capitalism*, a polemic published in early 1917, Lenin argued that the New Imperialism was the natural result of that imperative, as each country sought to establish exclusive foreign domains for its own domestic investors. After the success of the Bolshevik revolution in Russia, Lenin's views quickly became the prevailing Marxist orthodoxy. For several decades, the straight Leninist line remained the sole authority on the subject for Marxists everywhere, including the United States.

Marxists in America

In time, however, a new element was added concerning the form of control exercised by the colonial powers at the core of the global system. Lenin, having died well before the ebbing of the New Imperialism, could not have anticipated the wave of decolonization that was to sweep the map after World War II, creating dozens of new states across Africa, Asia, and other peripheral regions. Yet such an historic development could hardly be ignored by his followers. The question had to be answered: how could capitalism continue to sustain itself in the absence of formal empires? The only remedy that seemed possible was the substitution of *informal* empires. Control of the periphery must still exist, only now it was exercised informally, not formally, through relations of trade and investment. Colonialism was simply replaced by neocolonialism – modern economic imperialism (or neo-imperialism).

In Marxist circles in the United States, the new line of argument emphasized above all the symbiotic relationship between giant multinational corporations and their home governments – not surprising given the fact that at the time the world's largest private enterprises were almost all US-based. For partisans like Paul Baran and Paul Sweezy (1966) or

Harry Magdoff (1969), the key to explaining the persistence of economic imperialism lay in the traditional capitalist imperative of expansion. There was no need to invoke an alleged secular decline in the rate of profit. Overproduction or underconsumption were not the problem. All that mattered was the modern corporation's basic interest in survival, which appeared to leave it no choice but to extend the scope of its market continually and to be looking always for new sources of supply. Its compulsion was to maximize its market power in the grinding competitive struggle. This in turn led enterprises to call for the support of their national government, which was induced to play an active role on their behalf. As Magdoff put it, this is "the reality of imperialism." The principal characteristic of the capitalist system was now the "competition among groups of giant corporations and their governments [which] takes place over the entire globe . . . Imperialism is not a matter of choice for a capitalist society; it is the way of life of such a society" (Magdoff 1969: 14, 15, 26).

What was the impact of this "reality?" Gradually, attention shifted from explaining the origins of the new form of imperialism to analyzing its consequences, in particular for the poverty-stricken peoples of the periphery. Ironically, classical Marxism had been relatively optimistic on prospects for peripheral regions, stressing the positive effects of trade and investment. Economic relations with the metropolitan center were expected to accelerate the development of less advanced areas. Even Lenin concurred, arguing that transfers of capital and technology from the core would ultimately establish a viable and dynamic industrial base in the periphery. The revolutionary leader further expected that these transfers would eventually lead to a decline into decadence and atrophy by the imperialist powers themselves, as the capitalist class grew more and more dependent on *rentier* earnings from its overseas investments. According to Lenin, this was all part of the dialectical process of mature capitalist development. He called it the system's stage of "parasitism and decay" (Lenin 1917: 118).

However, that was not the view of Lenin's later followers in the United States, who stressed the negative rather than the positive effects of core–periphery relations. Neocolonialism was expected to block, not promote, the development of the poor. Worse, it could actually be said to *generate* a condition of poverty by locking peripheral regions into terms of "unequal exchange." As theorist Andre Gunder Frank (1966) put it, the condition of the periphery was not just what might be called "*un*development." Rather it should be called "*under*development," a form of poverty *imposed* on the poor by their economic relations with the rich. Poor countries were not poor because they had always been that way. It was because they were *made* that way. Their production structures were systematically distorted and subordinated by the economies of the metropolitan center – what Gunder Frank called "the development of underdevelopment." For American Marxists, the challenge was to find ways to ameliorate the persistent poverty of the periphery.

A new faction

The historical materialism of Marxism was by no means the sole source of inspiration for the Left-Out. Also influential were selected non-Marxist writers who were prepared to challenge mainstream orthodoxy. An early inspiration was the English journalist John Hobson (1902), who after covering the Boer War in South Africa published an impassioned critique of European empire building that is now remembered as the first formal statement of a theory of economic imperialism. Even more impact came from the work of the Hungarian economic historian Karl Polanyi, whose classic treatise *The Great Transformation* (1944) offered lasting insights on the social foundations of markets. Polanyi today is best remembered for his cultural approach to economics, a point of view that in his day was alien to conventional economists but later became enormously popular among sociologists and historians. Additional inspiration came from the revisionist school of American foreign economic policy, starting with William Appleman Williams's landmark volume on *The Tragedy of American Diplomacy* (1959), which in turn led to Fred Block's heterodox interpretation of monetary history in *The Origins of International Economic Disorder* (1977).

Similarly influential was so-called dependency theory, an effort to explain the persistent poverty of peripheral regions that first emerged in Latin America in the 1950s. (I will have more to say on dependency theory in Chapter 7.) Classical sociology played a role in highlighting how international inequalities and hierarchies could be socially structured. So too did the so-called Annales School of historiography in France, with its emphasis on long-term processes of social development. Common to all these influences was an emphasis on looking at the totality of society in historical context, making use of ideas and insights from any or all of the social sciences.

Especially important also was the intellectual tradition known as critical theory, broadly conceived as a form of inquiry aimed at attaining human emancipation. The goal is to decrease domination and increase freedom in all forms. Given its many variants, critical theory is not easily characterized. Encompassed by the term are diverse variations on Marxist or neo-Marxist themes as well as all kinds of other heterodox schools of thought. One sympathetic source suggests that a more adequate label would be "ideologically oriented inquiry" (Griffiths 1999: 114). The common denominator, according to another commentary, is an "oppositional frame of mind" (Brown 2001: 192). Critical theory challenges orthodoxies of every sort and is particularly averse to modern capitalism in all its guises. Critical theorists may not agree on what they are for, but they surely know what they are against. As a placard in a London May Day demonstration once proclaimed: "Capitalism should be replaced by something nicer."

From all these diverse roots sprang the Left-Out, a new faction within the invisible college of IPE that is quite distinct from the mainstream US version of the field – a branch not of political science but, rather, based more in the discipline of sociology. The central characteristic of heterodox scholarship is its emphasis on ambitious questions of systemic transformation in historical context – what one sympathizer has labeled a "historical-relativist paradigm . . . drawn from an eclectic mix of factors" (Tooze 1985: 121). A wide-band historical-relativist paradigm contrasts sharply with the more fine-grained focus of the orthodox American school, where broader structures are rarely problematized. With its penchant for mid-level theory, the American school tends to ignore the Big Picture. The Left-Out do not ignore the Big Picture, they embrace it.

Nowhere is the difference between the two camps more evident than in their contrasting approaches to the controversial topic of globalization. In its economic dimension, globalization is equated with an increasingly close integration of national markets. For the Left-Out, this development represents a fundamental transformation of economic geography, eroding the distinctiveness of the state. In place of territorially distinct economies, we are said to be moving toward a more unified world model, a truly *global* marketplace, with its own unique structures, processes, and actors – in short, a dramatically new spatial organization of economic activity. In the words of one of the Left-Out's most prominent figures: "Globalization represents a new stage in the evolving world capitalist system . . . the near-culmination of a centuries-long process of the spread of capitalist production around the world" (Robinson 2004: 2). Heterodox scholars often differ over what this new stage will ultimately mean for us. However, with only rare exceptions, they all seem to agree that something truly historic is happening. An illustrative collection of essays offering a diversity of perspectives on the globalization phenomenon is provided by Richard Appelbaum and William Robinson (2005).

In the orthodox American school, by contrast, there is considerably more skepticism. Globalization, it is felt, is overhyped, more a buzzword than a breakthrough – just so much "globaloney," or maybe even "globaloony." That something significant may be going on in the world is acknowledged. Indeed, it is hard to miss the degree to which interdependence among national economies has spread and accelerated in the current era. However, for most in the mainstream, that is simply more of the same process of economic integration that has been going on for decades – a fashionable new label for a hoary old trend. The sovereign state remains the central actor. As Keohane and Nye (2012: xxiii) put it in the latest edition of an earlier landmark book, "globalization refers to an intensification of what we described as interdependence in 1977."

To a large extent, the contrast between the two approaches is a natural result of their separate disciplinary heritages. For the American school, with its roots in the political science subfield of IR, a pronounced emphasis on the state and inter-state relations is only to be expected. For heterodox scholars, by contrast, with their interest in broader social systems and history, a more holistic view seems apt. The two branches are simply asking different kinds of questions.

In one respect, however, they are remarkably alike. In each case there is widespread consensus on a common analytical framework to structure and guide research – what might be called their foundational models. For more orthodox US scholars, as indicated, the foundational model is Open Economy Politics. For most of the Left-Out, it goes by the name of world-systems theory.

World-systems theory

World-systems theory represents a multidisciplinary and macro-scale approach to the study of IPE. In ontological terms the focus is on entire inter-societal systems ("world-systems"), not just sovereign states, as the fundamental unit of inquiry. Analysis looks at human institutions over long periods of time and employs the broadest possible geographical domain. The purpose of research is to elucidate the causes and consequences of social change, understood to involve the evolution of world-systems in historical perspective.

The modern world-system

Generically, world-systems are conceived as comprehensive human interaction networks, encompassing everything from the individual and the household to national and global markets. The specific system that prevails today, the *modern* world-system, has origins that date back to the sixteenth century. The modern world-system is understood as a stratified and long-lasting structure composed of three distinct tiers: a dominant core along with dependent peripheral and semi-peripheral regions. The dynamics of the modern world-system, it is assumed, are driven primarily by the dual forces of capitalism and geopolitics, where corporations and governments compete vigorously for power and wealth. Competition among firms and states, in turn, is conditioned by an ongoing struggle among classes and by the resistance of peripheral and semi-peripheral peoples to domination and exploitation from the core. No political center exists compared with past systems like the Roman Empire. The modern world-system is identified with the global market economy and is ruled by capitalist modes of production and exchange. Its discipline comes from the functional specialization of the separate tiers operating within an institutionally stabilized division of labor.

Credit for first systematically codifying the world-systems approach is usually given to the sociologist Immanuel Wallerstein, starting with the first volume of a monumental multivolume treatise on *The Modern World-System* (Wallerstein 1974). Already, before him, Marxist analysis and dependency theory each had promoted the idea of a stratified world divided between a dominant core and a dependent periphery. To this perspective Wallerstein added much nuance, including the fresh notion of a semi-periphery that mediates between the other two tiers. Found in the semi-periphery are the larger countries of the developing world such as what today we call the BRICs (Brazil, Russia, India, and China), along with other smaller countries at an intermediate level of development such as Chile, Thailand, and Turkey. While the core enjoys a high level of technological development, selling sophisticated high-value goods and services, the role of the periphery is to supply raw materials, foodstuffs, and cheap labor on a basis of unequal exchange. Between them, the semi-periphery benefits from exploiting the periphery even as it is itself exploited by the core.

Following Wallerstein, others sought to add their own twist to the approach. World-systems theory too, like the mainstream American school, has had its successive generations, although without a comparable hardening of methodology. Joining Wallerstein in a First Generation were expansive thinkers like Christopher Chase-Dunn, who founded both a new Institute for Research on World-Systems (at the University of California, Riverside) and a new publishing venue, the *Journal of World-System Research*, which is now the official journal of the Political Economy of the World-System section of the American Sociological Association. In 1991 Chase-Dunn published *Global Formation: Structures of the World Economy* (1991), a major synthesis and restatement of the world-systems approach, which has since become a standard reference work for the Left-Out. A Second Generation, coming to maturity in the 1990s and beyond, included such major contributors as Robert Denemark, William Robinson, Mark Rupert, and Beverly Silver, each with a distinct research agenda. While Robinson stressed the need to return to the Left-Out's Marxist roots, Denemark concentrated largely on intellectual history, Rupert on issues of economic hegemony and imperialism, and Silver on labor relations. Also of note is Craig Murphy, an influential voice on governance and global inequality. Although less closely identified with world-systems theory than others of his generation, Murphy is no less committed to the Left-Out's passion for heterodox theory and radical social change. Further diversity is now being added by an emerging Third Generation, which is still working out its own perspectives and priorities.

Debates

Overall, the modern world-system is assumed to have great staying power. It has, after all, already survived for centuries. Its essential character remains the same, always a hierarchy of three tiers sustained by the forces of global capitalism. However, that does not mean that the structure is considered to be in any sense static or immobile – quite the contrary in fact. Heterodox scholars take for granted that, within the broad outlines of the modern world-system, much room is left for transformation of key features over time. Individual countries or regions may move up or down from one tier to another; mobility in either direction is possible. The tiers themselves may fragment or be reconfigured in various ways. The nature of the dynamics linking the three tiers may evolve substantially as well. History is presumed to proceed in stages, sometimes gradually and at times in great waves. Social change is the rule, not the exception.

Not surprisingly, therefore, debates emerge over all sorts of issues, just as they do among mainstream US scholars. The Left-Out are no more monolithic than the orthodox American school, despite consensus on the fundamentals of paradigm and agenda. Consider, for example, the question of the role of the state in the modern world-system. For Wallerstein and many others, states remain central actors despite the globalization of economic activity. National governments still play a crucial role, seeking to ensure the viability of their leading market sectors through such means as trade controls and industrial policy (Wallerstein 2004). For a more Marxist-leaning scholar like Robinson, by contrast, such "state-centric" thinking is misguided. The global system, Robinson maintains, is now dominated by a transnational capitalist class. National governments have become no more than that class's subservient agents (Robinson 2004, 2008).

Also like the orthodox American school, the scope of heterodox scholarship is broad. While some theorists, notably Robinson and Chase-Dunn, set their sights high, probing the question of systemic transformation in the most sweeping historical terms, others concentrate on more specific policy challenges such as global governance (Murphy 1994) or economic development (McMichael 2008). Some explore the intellectual origins of the world-systems view (Denemark 1999) or the ideologies of globalization (Rupert 2000); others analyze the forms of struggle of those who have resisted domination and exploitation (Silver 2003). Yet others, more narrowly, pick apart the notion of capitalism to focus on specific aspects of market activity such as, for example, agricultural trade or bond finance. As in the mainstream US tradition, within its preferred ontology the Left-Out's agenda knows few bounds.

Pride and prejudice

Like their counterparts in the American school, the Left-Out take pride in the way their version of IPE has developed. In their case too, pride is by no means misplaced. The Left-Out's take on the field also offers advantages – above all, a perspective on the Big Picture that is so glaringly absent from the OEP paradigm. One does not have to agree with every – or even any – element of world-systems theory to appreciate the effort to push discourse beyond the mid-level. Why should the state necessarily be prioritized for purposes of analysis? Why should the broader structure of global relations not be problematized? Why must holistic thinking be avoided? Further, much can be said for Left-Out's normative spirit, which seeks to give social purpose to serious scholarship. Objective observation need not be the sole reason for research.

Yet among mainstream scholars in the United States the efforts of the Left-Out are treated with indifference, if not outright disdain. In part this is purely a matter of prejudice. Political scientists may have an inferiority complex when it comes to economics, but quite the reverse is true concerning how sociology and other "lesser" social sciences are regarded. These disciplines, typically, are seen as often even less "professional" in their standards. Heterodox scholars feel obliged to keep up with the latest developments in the American school, if only to know what they oppose. Mainstream research is often included in their course syllabi and referenced in their published work. The compliment, however, is rarely repaid by more orthodox academics, many of whom are not even aware that an alternative version of IPE exists just next door. In writing my *Intellectual History*, I was by no means the first to leave out the Left-Out.

In part also, heterodox scholarship is avoided because of lingering associations with Marxism, which remains a suspect tradition in most of US academia. When the modern field of IPE was first getting started in the United States, any mention of Marxism or other leftist doctrines was discouraged by the chilling effect of post-World War II anti-communism. That effect has lasted, refusing to fade away even after the end of the Cold War. To this day, few American scholars have much taste for ideas or arguments that might smack of anti-capitalist sentiment.

Most important, however, is a fundamental disagreement about epistemology. Mainstream scholars simply have little tolerance for an analytical approach that is so infuriatingly at variance with their own intellectual preferences. The grand visions offered by a historical-relativist paradigm, dense with sociological detail, do not fit easily with hypothetico-deductivism, the reductionist methodology favored by the

American school. Heterodoxy is too prone to unsubstantiated general-ization and too lacking in systematic evaluation of evidence. Because of the high degree of historical contingency in world-systems theory, it is difficult to reduce insights to a concise set of logical theorems. Because of the lengthy time perspective of the analysis, spanning decades and even centuries, it is difficult to convert conclusions into empirically falsifiable propositions; and because of a common propensity to mix positivist observation and normative judgments, it is difficult even to assess the fundamental soundness of the Left-Out's reasoning. For most mainstream scholars, the arguments of heterodox theorists are simply not persuasive.

The result, regrettably, is best summarized by a famous line in the 1967 film *Cool Hand Luke*: "What we've got here is failure to communi-cate." Direct engagement between the two styles of IPE is rare. Mostly, the two branches of the invisible college in the United States simply go their separate ways, in mutual disregard – a dialogue of the deaf, not unlike the deep void between international economics and IR that Strange wrote about back in 1970 (Strange 1970). Insularity reigns in both cohorts. Little attempt is made to learn from each other.

References

Appelbaum, Richard P. and William I. Robinson (eds) (2005), *Critical Globalization Studies*, London: Routledge.

Baran, Paul A. and Paul M. Sweezy (1966), *Monopoly Capital*, New York: Monthly Review Press.

Block, Fred (1977), *The Origins of International Economic Disorder: A Study of United States International Monetary Policy from World War II to the Present*, Berkeley, CA: University of California Press.

Brown, Christopher (2001), "'Our side?' Critical theory and international relations," in R. Wyn Jones (ed.), *Critical Theory and World Politics*, Boulder, CO: Lynne Rienner, pp. 191–204.

Chase-Dunn, Christopher K. (1991), *Global Formation: Structures of the World Economy*, New York: Basic Blackwell.

Cohen, Benjamin J. (1973), *The Question of Imperialism: The Political Economy of Dominance and Dependence*, New York: Basic Books.

Denemark, Robert A. (1999), "World system history: from traditional international poli-tics to the study of global relations," *International Studies Review*, **1** (2), 43–75.

Frank, Andre Gunder (1966), *The Development of Underdevelopment*, New York: Monthly Review Press.

Griffiths, Martin (1999), *Fifty Great Thinkers in International Relations*, New York: Routledge.

Hobson, John A. (1902), *Imperialism: A Study*, London: J. Nisbet.

Keohane, Robert O. and Joseph S. Nye Jr (2012), *Power and Interdependence*, fourth edition, Boston, MA: Longman.

Lenin, V.I. (1917), *Imperialism: The Highest Stage of Capitalism*, Petrograd: Parus.

Magdoff, Harry (1969), *The Age of Imperialism*, New York: Monthly Review Press.

McMichael, Philip (2008), *Development and Social Change: A Global Perspective*, fourth edition, Thousand Oaks, CA: Pine Forge Press.

Murphy, Craig N. (1994), *Industrial Organization and Industrial Change: Global Governance since 1850*, London: Policy Press.

Murphy, Craig N. (2011), "Do the Left-Out matter?," in Nicola Phillips and Catherine E. Weaver (eds), *International Political Economy: Debating the Past, Present and Future*, London: Routledge, pp. 160–168.

Polanyi, Karl (1944), *The Great Transformation: The Political and Economic Origins of Our Time*, Boston, MA: Beacon Press.

Robinson, William I. (2004), *A Theory of Global Capitalism: Production, Class, and State in a Transnational World*, Baltimore, MD: Johns Hopkins University Press.

Robinson, William I. (2008), *Latin America and Global Capitalism: A Critical Globalization Perspective*, Baltimore, MD: Johns Hopkins University Press.

Rupert, Mark (2000), *Ideologies of Globalization: Contending Visions of a New World Order*, London: Routledge.

Silver, Beverly J. (2003), *Forces of Labor: Workers' Movements and Globalization since 1870*, New York: Cambridge University Press.

Strange, Susan (1970), "International economics and international relations: a case of mutual neglect," *International Affairs*, **46** (2), 304–315.

Tooze, Roger (1985), "International political economy," in Steve Smith (ed.), *International Relations: British and American Perspectives*, Oxford: Basil Blackwell, pp. 108–125.

Wallerstein, Immanuel M. (1974), *The Modern World-System*, Volume 1, New York: Academic Press. (Subsequent volumes published in 1980, 1989, and 2011.)

Wallerstein, Immanuel M. (2004), *World-Systems Analysis: An Introduction*, Durham, NC: Duke University Press.

Williams, William Appleman (1959), *The Tragedy of American Diplomacy*, New York: Norton.

4 The British school

Across the Atlantic from the United States we find an even more prominent alternative to the orthodox American school, the branch of the invisible college that in my *Intellectual History* I called the British school of IPE. Apart from the United States, there is no place in the world with more specialists working the field than the UK – perhaps 10 percent of the global total, as compared with half in the United States (Sharman and Weaver 2013). In Britain too, a broad institutionalized network of experts has come into being with its own distinctive features and perspectives. If there is a principal rival to the American school, it is the British school.

The contrasts between the two schools could not be more striking. The transatlantic divide (Cohen 2007) is real. The characteristic British style has much more in common with America's Left-Out than with the mainstream US version of the field. From the perspective of the American school, the British faction too deserves to be called "heterodox" or "radical."

In the British style, as among the Left-Out, scholars work from a distinctly different vision of how the world works and how it should be evaluated. Reflecting Britain's traditional intellectual culture, as noted in Chapter 1, the study of IPE generally tends to throw off the "shackles of methodological nationalism." In British ontology, no one unit of analysis is prioritized above all others. Research also tends to be more inclusive and multidisciplinary in scope than in the US mainstream. No academic specialization is ignored if it is thought to add value to analysis. IPE is conceived as a true interdiscipline, open to insights from many other areas of inquiry.

The British school is also more normative in ambition, again like America's Left-Out. As compared with the US mainstream, scholarship tends to be more critical of established orthodoxies and more engaged with social issues, more impatient with the status quo and more eager to change attitudes or practices. The British school's world view is anything but dispassionate. The problematique of the field is ecumenical, concerned with all manner of social and ethical issues. The main purpose of research is judgment: to identify injustice. The driving ambition is amelioration: to make the world a better place. Where the mainstream American school aspires to the objectivity of conventional US social science, the British school is openly normative in the tradition of classical moral philosophy.

Correspondingly, analytical methods are anything but reductionist. Scholarship tends to be more qualitative than in the orthodox US style, attaching less importance to narrow hypothesis testing or systematic evaluation of hard evidence. Work is typically more interpretive in tone and more institutional and historical in nature. Scientific method is valued less than a broad organic comprehension of "society" – the social context of IPE. Where the American school self-consciously restricts itself mainly to mid-level theorizing, the British school aims for grander visions of structural transformation or social development. The central focus is on coming to grips with the great issues of life.

Intellectual influences

If this introductory sketch of the British school seems to bear more than a passing resemblance to America's Left-Out, it is no accident. The two camps have far more in common with one another than either does with the orthodox US mainstream. Both are more inclined toward a historical-relativist paradigm, rejecting the "shackles of methodological nationalism." Both are more inclusive and more normative, and both are impatient with the hard science model that is so prized by the American school.

The two, however, are by no means identical. There are also significant differences, reflecting somewhat divergent intellectual legacies. Although they are undeniably both part of the same family tree, their relationship is more like that of first cousins than siblings. For the Left-Out, nineteenth-century Marxism was a dominant – albeit not exclusive – source of inspiration, evident still in a pronounced antipathy for capitalism. The taproot of the British school, by contrast, goes further back, to the classical political economy of the eighteenth century, with that movement's broad inclusiveness and links to moral philosophy. We know that many of the best-known classical political economists were British, from Adam Smith onwards. Echoes of their thinking have continued to linger down through the years in the country's scholarly community. Less emphasis is placed on the evils of global capitalism.

The two cousins are also separated by the distinctively different historical experiences of their respective countries of origin. America's Left-Out could hardly fail to be influenced by what they saw as the hegemonic, not to say "imperial," role of the United States in the post-World War II era. Much of their radicalism is driven by a distaste for America's role at the peak of the capitalist system. British scholars, by contrast, live in a post-colonial nation that has clearly suffered a great come-down since its days as the center of an empire on which the sun never set. Decolonization and economic decline have been among the major drivers of the study of IPE in Britain (Clift and Rosamond 2009).

In practice, the contours of the British school are due most of all to the dominating influence of two scholars in particular – the Englishwoman Susan Strange and Robert Cox, a Canadian. Their respective roles in shaping the field in Britain, since the rebirth of IPE in the 1970s, are unmatched. Together, they are responsible for what have become some of the most characteristic features of today's British school. Significantly, neither was trained in political science, unlike all the best known pioneers of IPE in the United States. Strange's degree was in economics, and Cox's in history.

Susan Strange

Strange's role began with her stirring 1970 manifesto, "International economics and international relations: a case of mutual neglect" (Strange 1970) which, in uncompromising terms, laid out the case for a more modern approach to the study of international economic relations. However, it was hardly her only contribution, as I indicated in my *Intellectual History*. Over the next three decades, until her untimely death in 1998, she provided the bold and effective leadership needed to build a new field of IPE in Britain. Today she is revered as the patron saint of the British school. In the words of one prominent scholar (Langley 2009: 127), "the research and writings of Susan Strange came to frame the intellectual trajectory of British IPE," or as another once put it to me in private correspondence, "She founded IPE as we know it here in Britain and she left a great hole in it when she left."

For example, quickly following her manifesto, Strange moved to create an institutional vehicle to help promote the "bridge-building" between international economics and international relations that she was so ardently advocating. This was the International Political Economy Group (IPEG), now an established section of the British International Studies Association (BISA) playing a role comparable to that of the APSA's Political Economy Section or the ISA's International Political Economy Section in the United States. At the time, IPEG was the world's first organized IPE research network. The aim of IPEG was to bring together scholars, journalists, and policy-makers for regular discussions of issues of the world economy. For fans of the British School, choosing to ignore parallel developments then occurring on the other side of the Atlantic, this truly was the moment of modern IPE's birth. Declares one source flatly: "Today's field of international political economy can be traced back to 1971, when Susan Strange . . . founded the International Political Economy Group" (Murphy and Nelson 2001: 393).

Even more importantly, Strange led with her writings, which were prolific. By her own admission, she was not much of a theorist. Her aim, according to two admirers, was not "to develop a full theory of IPE, but a way of thinking, a framework for thinking" (Tooze and May 2002: 15). Four themes, in particular, shone through her work, each becoming a hallmark of the British version of the field.

First was an emphasis on inclusiveness – as much openness of inquiry as possible. Scholarly ecumenism was a persistent refrain in her writing. "International political economy is still unfenced, still open to all comers," she declared in 1984. "It ought . . . to remain so" (Strange 1984: ix). Likewise, in 1991, she advised that "the study of international political economy would do well to stay as an open range, like the old Wild West, accessible . . . to literate people of all walks of life" (Strange 1991: 33). She firmly abhorred any artificial constraints on research. Leading by example, she freely crossed academic boundaries in pursuit of her scholarly interests, vigorously touting the advantages of multidisciplinarity. Others in the British tradition have eagerly followed, aiming in effect to resurrect the broader, more inclusive perspectives of classical political economy. Many British scholars even promote the alternative term Global Political Economy, rather than IPE, in order to highlight their preference for a more holistic approach to the subject.

Second was an intense engagement with social issues. What was the point of intellectual inquiry, she asked, if not to right the wrongs of the world? Distributional considerations in particular were always on her mind, whether speaking of the pursuit of wealth or the pursuit of power. The key question was always: *Cui bono*? For whose good? Nor did she shy away from judgments about matters of ethics or equity. For her, scholarship was inseparable from values. She loved to remind everyone of the link that had long existed between classical political economy and the study of moral philosophy, prior to the fragmentation of the social sciences that began in the nineteenth century. That link, she felt, needed to be revived. IPE should be "about justice, as well as efficiency: about order and national identity and cohesion, even self-respect, as well as about cost and price" (Strange 1984: x). True to her beliefs, she continually dared colleagues to make moral judgments.

Third was her unmistakable impatience with "The Establishment," as she put it, which led her to adopt a skeptical attitude toward orthodoxy of any kind. She was an iconoclast and radical with an instinctive sympathy for the ambitions of traditional critical theory. Although unencumbered by any specific ideology, she too aimed to decrease domination and increase freedom in all forms. One of the principle purposes of IPE, she argued repeatedly, was "to question authority, whether political or academic" (Strange 1995: 295). She could certainly be said to have an oppositional frame of mind. Manifest throughout her *oeuvre* was a strong distaste for anything that might be regarded as mainstream thinking – especially mainstream *American* thinking. She was a constant critic of what she saw as the stultifying narrowness of the American version of IPE, with its state-centric ontology rooted in the international relations branch of political science. IR, she argued, should be viewed as a subset of IPE, not the other way around:

> The whole point of studying international political economy rather than international relations is to extend more widely the conventional limits of the study of politics, and the conventional concepts of who engages in politics, and of how and by whom power is exercised to influence outcomes. Far from being a subdiscipline of international relations, IPE should claim that international relations are a subdiscipline of IPE. (Strange 1994: 218)

This did not mean that Strange was somehow anti-American. In fact, in many ways she truly admired the United States – the only country, she once noted, where you can buy a tee shirt emblazoned with her favorite slogan, "Question Authority" (Strange 1995: 295). Yet this did not stop her from being offended by what she saw as the intellectual myopia of American academics, whom she attacked with unrestrained glee. Once she publicly challenged a respected US professor to "wake up" and face the facts (Strange 1994). All this found a ready audience among British scholars, many of whom were understandably eager to find an alternative to what one source described as the "self-identified US 'supremacy'" in the field of IPE (Murphy and Tooze 1991: 17). Another source suggested that Strange's "stinging criticism of US intellectual trends provided room for British scholars and students to ask different types of questions and use different methodologies from their US counterparts" (O'Brien and Williams 2010: 39).

Finally, there was Strange's passion, which suffused everything she undertook. This was not a person who could do things by half. Passion was evident in the wide range of issues she chose to take on, from the decline of Britain's pound sterling to the rise of globalization. It could be found in her confrontational, in-your-face approach to academic debate and teaching. To be a serious scholar, she told her students, you must have "fire in the belly." Most of all, it was manifest in her prose, which made even the dreariest subjects come vividly alive. Passion is not a word normally associated with the kind of parsimonious, positivist analysis encouraged by the American school. Even after Strange's passing, though, passion remains a central characteristic of the contrasting British approach to IPE.

Robert Cox

The other great influence on British IPE was Robert Cox, a more coolly cerebral Canadian with a particular interest – reflecting his professional training – in history. Like America's Left-Out, he was driven by a commitment to historical materialism. He too thought in terms of a succession of vast and complex historical structures defined by their modes of production, which he chose to call "world orders." Just as Wallerstein's world-systems theory became the foundational model for America's Left-Out, Cox's notion of world orders became the foundational model for the British school.

Unlike Strange, Cox did consider himself a theorist, and his theories, encouraging interpretative historical analysis, have shaped generations of scholarship in Britain since they were first enunciated in the early 1980s. Although largely ignored by the American school, his writings are still widely taught and debated in British universities. Today Cox is revered as second only to Strange in the pantheon of the British school. "The work of Robert Cox," remarks one observer, "has inspired many students to rethink the way in which we study international political economy, and it is fair to say that [his] historical materialism is perhaps the most important alternative to realist and liberal perspectives in the field today" (Griffiths 1999: 118). Numerous sources cite Cox as the starting point for their own theoretical studies (for example, Gill and Law 1989; Palan and Gills 1994).

For Cox, the purpose of IPE was nothing less than to understand "the structures that underlie the world" (Cox 1999: 390). His breakthrough came in 1981 with publication of an article entitled "Social forces, states, and world orders: beyond international relations theory" (Cox 1981), a paper that has since attained virtually iconic status among British scholars. Although much more was to come later, including his monumental *Production, Power, and World Order* (Cox 1987), nothing else matched the impact of that early, innovative essay. Changes were occurring in the world economy, he contended, that were truly profound and needed to be seen in their totality. At issue was nothing less than the emergence of a new world order, a new historical structure reflecting an expansion and integration of production processes on a transnational scale. Central to it all was a transformative realignment of social forces – a new "global class structure alongside or superimposed on national class structures" (Cox 1981: 147).

Cox's starting point was a distinction, noted back in Chapter 1, between positivist social science – what he called "problem-solving" theory – and critical theory. For Cox, the principal difference between the two had to do with the dimension of time. As he saw it, the perspective of problem-solving theory, by which he meant most of what is done in the American school, is relatively short term. In effect, he said, problem-solving theory timidly assumes that the major components of a system, including above all states, are not subject to fundamental change. Cox was among the first to indict the US style of IPE for taking broader structures for granted. Underlying frameworks, he complained, are simply treated as parameters, a kind of "continuing present" (Cox 1981: 129), fixing the limits within which action occurs. The approach, therefore, is essentially ahistorical. Analysis focuses on the action, not the limits. Solutions are sought within the existing system.

Critical theory, by contrast, deliberately adopts a much lengthier time horizon, measured not in months or years but in decades, even generations. As indicated in the last chapter, critical theory had already been around for some time. Cox, however, put a particular spin on it. For him, what most distinguished critical theory was that it steps outside the confines of existing relationships to highlight a system's origins and, above all, its development potential. The approach's main value lies in the fact that it is anything but ahistorical; structures are anything but parameters. In Cox's words: "Critical theory is theory of history in the sense of being concerned not just with the past but with a continuing process of historical change" (Cox 1981: 129). Inquiry can focus on how systems came into being in the past, what changes are presently occurring within them, and how those changes might be shaped in the future. What are the sources of tension in a system, and what patterns of change are possible? In short, critical theory allows one to think seriously about systemic transformation.

Most importantly, for Cox, critical theory allows one to be *critical*. Instead of taking prevailing institutions and power relationships for granted, it questions them. Instead of disaggregating issues to make them more analytically tractable, it keeps attention focused on the system as a whole, seeking out sources of contradiction and conflict. Problem-solving theory, in his view, was conservative – implicitly favoring the status quo – since it does not question the underlying interests that are served by a given structure. Problem-solving theory, he insisted, was about managing the world as it is, not changing it. Critical theory, by contrast, directly "allows for a normative choice in favor of a social and political order different from the prevailing order" (Cox 1981: 130). For Cox, as for Strange, the key question was: *Cui bono?*

The answer, he felt, was to be found in the concept of "world orders," historical structures that he saw as a function of three broad categories of influences: material capabilities, ideas, and institutions. Material capabilities, as reflected in technological capacities and modes of production, were rapidly becoming integrated across national frontiers; and the accelerating internationalization of production, in turn, was generating new inter-subjective understandings of social relations and new innovations in governing institutions. Profound change was occurring, with unmistakable distributional implications.

How would it all turn out? In assessing future world order prospects, Cox rejected the narrow state-centrism of traditional IR theory. The state could not be analyzed in isolation. Historical change had to be thought of in terms of the reciprocal relationship of structures and actors within a much broader conceptualization of international relations, the "state–society complex." Outcomes would depend on the response of "social forces," defined as the main collective actors engendered by the relations of production both within and across all spheres of activity. "International production," he wrote, "is mobilizing social forces, and it is through these forces that its major political consequences *vis-à-vis* the nature of states and future world orders may be anticipated" (Cox 1981: 147). The overriding imperative was to support social forces that would "bargain for a better deal within the world economy" (Cox 1981: 151).

However, it is instructive that Cox also rejected the rigid stratifications of world-systems theory, despite the evident commonalities with his own approach. Like America's Left-Out, Cox owes much to the dialecticism of Marxist analysis, with its emphasis on the internal dynamics of systemic transformation. Both world-systems theory and the notion of world orders assume that change can only be understood dialectically, with each successive structure generating the contradictions that bring about its future development. Each also draws inspiration from Polanyi's *The Great Transformation* (1944), which placed systemic evolution center stage and was unabashedly normative in tone. Yet for Cox, world-systems theory, with its formulaic three-tiered structure, was simply too confining. His own approach, with its state–society complex and social forces, was far more eclectic, defying easy classification. Strange may have put it best when she called him an "eccentric," although quickly adding "in the best English sense of the word, a loner, a fugitive from intellectual camps" (Strange 1988: 269–270).

Contrasts

It may be an exaggeration to suggest that the British school has defined itself simply by its opposition to mainstream thought in the United States, along lines legitimized by Strange and Cox. However, that would not be entirely inaccurate either. The differences between the two camps are legion. Winston Churchill, echoing an earlier thought of George Bernard Shaw, said that America and Britain are two nations divided by a common language. The American and British schools of IPE, in similar fashion, have come to be two factions divided by a common subject.

In fact, for many scholars in Britain, an adversarial attitude toward scholarship on the other side of the Atlantic has been a chief source of inspiration. Not at all unusual was an influential broadside published a few years back that labeled the US version of IPE "a vulgar, fraudulent discipline . . . a crude amalgam of neoclassical economics, pluralist domestic political science, and realist international relations theory . . . We can only wonder why the tradition of classical political economy is passed over in such haste . . . The Americans fail to grasp the complex organic set of social relations which is the global political economy" (Burnham 1994: 221–222). Although not all British scholars would express themselves with quite so much vinegar, it is clear that most take pride in the contrasts between their own style of IPE and the orthodox US version.

The differences have been characterized in many ways. Three examples should suffice. First is Mark Blyth, a Scot by birth who teaches in the United States and feels himself caught in the middle of British and American IPE, "torn between two lovers" (Blyth 2011). The contrast between the schools for him was brought home while attending two successive professional conferences, first in Britain and then in the United States. At the US meeting he found rigorous research papers on a wide variety of topics, most using sophisticated statistical techniques to test competing hypotheses and models. Yet, as is so often the case, conclusions were contingent at best and had to be couched in cautious, probabilistic terms. In the end he felt he was left with a lot of unanswered questions. At the British meeting, by contrast, he encountered a multitude of preconceived ideas, such as Marxism or world orders, that by definition provided a ready explanation for almost any subject – in his words, "a disciplinary monotheism that would make the US quants blush" (Blyth 2011: 138). In lieu of *unanswered questions*, he was met with a host of *unquestioned answers*. One side of the pond celebrates formal scientific method; on the other side, issues and ideology dominate.

Second is Catherine Weaver (2011), an American scholar, who likens the transatlantic divide to the well-known split between the two sides of the human brain. Science has long recognized that the right and left brains respond to the world in strikingly different ways, producing distinct personality types. A left-brain personality is rationalist, practical, and detail-oriented, more inclined to rely on objective linear logic. A right-brain personality, by contrast, is more interpretive and Big Picture oriented, and more reliant on emotions and intuition. Does this not seem to echo the contrasts between the two schools? In Weaver's words: "In a nutshell, the American school is deeply committed to the norms of science, carefully selecting and testing 'hard' data to provide persuasive causal explanations about the way the world *does* work. The British school is both more creative and risk-taking, aspiring to interpret political history and structures to say something powerful about the way the world *should* work" (Weaver 2011: 143). Despite the risk of caricature, the metaphor is apt.

Finally, we have Amanda Dickins, a Briton, who is particularly struck by the contrast between the positivism of the American school and the subjectivism of the critical theories favored by so many in the British school, with their disdain for strict rational choice. Britons do not always agree on what qualifies as "critical IPE," as noted recently by van Apeldorn *et al.* (2011). Critical theory, to repeat from the previous chapter, is a theme that comes in many variations. Some specialists prefer a narrow definition linking the approach closely to Marxism and historical materialism; others insist on a much broader oppositional style in the iconoclastic spirit of Strange. Representative of the diversity are two recent collections of essays by noted critical theorists (Shields *et al.* 2011; Belfrage and Worth 2012), united mainly in their passion to question the usefulness of rationalist causal models. Using a biological metaphor, Dickins amusingly defines the "diverse critical species that comprise the genus" of the British school as *Querimonia*, in contrast to the rationalist species *Ratiosuarus rex* that we know as the American school (Dickins 2006: 480).

Questions

In practical terms, we can see the divide between the two schools in their separate choices of what issues to address. Recall the suggestion that resistance to US intellectual trends gave British scholars room to ask distinctly different types of questions. Over the years, accordingly, their agenda has diverged considerably from the main concerns of the American school.

Problematique

For the US mainstream, as indicated, the core problematique encompasses two core questions: state behavior and system governance. For British scholars, that is far too narrow. Why, for example, in thinking about what actors do, should we limit ourselves just to *explaining* behavior? The American school's fascination with causal variables, in British eyes, pays undue deference to the principles of positivism and empiricism. IPE ought to be about more than formal modeling or hypothesis testing. It should also be about *evaluating* behavior and its consequences – about *normative* analysis. Scholars must do more than merely observe. In the spirit of what one source termed "the value-based tradition of classical political economy" (Watson 2005: 31), they must also *judge* – to denounce inequity and seek justice.

Likewise, in thinking about governance, why should analysis be limited just to economic relations? Why should theory be restricted just to what Cox called problem-solving within the existing system? IPE, for the British school, is about more than just the care and protection of economic interdependence. Much more fundamentally, it is about underlying social patterns and structures – about the way that society itself is ordered and governed, viewed in broad historical perspective. Here too inspiration comes ultimately from classical political economy. The world economy, it is said, cannot be studied on its own, apart from other social processes. Rather, it must be seen as embedded in a wider "social whole" (Krätke and Underhill 2006: 32), part of a broader conception of the totality of human experience. The goal of inquiry, concludes one source, is "to devise a programme giving a holistic account of the world we inhabit" (O'Brien 1995: 101).

On both questions, behavior and governance, the difference is not just about defining the basic units of analysis. The issue goes beyond ontology and has everything to do with the fundamental purpose of intellectual inquiry. All scholarship, presumably, is truth-seeking. However, whereas the American school aims to maintain a certain distance between the researcher and the subject of research, in hopes of preserving objectivity, the British school prefers to become fully engaged, in order to make the world a better place. Inquiry, in the words of Murphy and Tooze, is (or should be) about "the pursuit of the ethical life" (Murphy and Tooze 1991: 27). The aim is not just to *understand* but, where possible, to *improve*. That higher calling demands a problematique that is both normative in tone and universal in aspiration. Anything less may be dismissed as more or less idle chatter – in the worst sense of the term, merely "academic."

Traffic jam

Where, then, do we draw the line? If the agenda must be broadened, what else should be included? Strikingly, answers vary depending on taste, creating a traffic jam of competing research styles and programs. The British school, it turns out, has a lot of unanswered questions too.

In fact, the list of questions posed by the British school is remarkably long. Strange's call for an "open range" has been taken seriously by those who followed. Strange and Cox may be considered the First Generation of the British school. In a Second Generation, some scholars like Barry Gills concentrated on extending their kind of historical analysis of global systems. Others, however, branched out to take in a wider range of problems. Ronen Palan turned his attention to state theory and the changing modes of governance of the world economy. Roger Tooze explored the role of international business. Anthony Payne highlighted the complex politics of development, while Philip Cerny (a transplanted American) brought new dimensions to the analysis of global finance. In a Third Generation interests have spread even further. Matthew Watson has emphasized the historical roots of IPE, Nicola Phillips has renewed focus on development, Thomas Lawton has studied the evolving global production structure, and Timothy Sinclair has extended the study of international credit.

The result is an agenda that, admirably, is nothing if not ambitious – intellectual ecumenism taken to an extreme. Writes one source: "The inclusive approach . . . spreads wider than the issues of trade, investment and monetary relations. While not ignoring those issues, attention is paid to other aspects such as militarization, development, gender, and ecology" (O'Brien 1995: 98). Observes another: "British school IPE is characterized by a concern with direct analysis of issues in the world as they appear, such as globalization, finance, trade, inequality, poverty, production, gender, race, and so on" (Phillips 2005: 12). What could be more indicative of the school's commitment to openness than that final "and so on"? When one prominent scholar attempted to take stock of the field not long ago, he declared that "we can affirm a set of common concerns . . . global governance, global justice, development, poverty, inequality, and the roles of labour, social movements, women and the 'global South'" (Gills 2001: 234, 244). Little is left out when the subject is nothing less than the totality of human experience.

With so many questions, however, how does one begin to find answers? Inclusiveness may be a virtue but it can also lead to intellectual incoherence. Geoffrey Underhill, a leading voice in the field, is not alone in boasting that in its British version IPE "has long since burst the boundaries of traditional IR" (Underhill 2000: 815). Yet if the state-centric ontology of the US school is to be rejected, what is to replace it? Here too we have ecumenism taken to an extreme. While some, following Strange, would insist on the centrality of the individual as the primary unit of interest, others, following Cox, are happier with the study of historical structures. In between are all kinds of other candidates, from corporations and capitalists to classes or social forces. To say that the British school's ontology lacks a certain consonance would be a considerable understatement.

As even one the British school's most prominent partisans acknowledges, the school's ecumenicism is also "one of its weaknesses, in the sense that [the field's] boundaries can be notoriously hard to establish" (Phillips 2005: 10). Without established boundaries, there is no common agreement about what actors to look at or what relationships might take precedence – hence no firm basis for valid theory-building. Nor is there any common set of standards for evaluating processes or structures – and no firm basis for normative analysis either. Admirably high-minded judgments are offered in the name of justice or equity or empowerment, but on a basis that appears utterly subjective.

In short, we end up with a debilitating lack of focus. "A broad and somewhat inchoate field of study," is how one prominent figure ruefully describes the British version of IPE (Palan 2000: 2). British scholars seem at one in their resistance to the pretensions of the American school, but harmony breaks down when it comes to providing a compelling counterpoint.

Methods

We can also see the divide between the British and American schools in their respective choices of methodology. Resistance to US intellectual trends not only gave Britain's scholars room to ask different questions. It also gave them an excuse to use distinctly different approaches to research and analysis. Epistemology too has diverged considerably from the main techniques of the American school.

For Britain's scholars, an inclusive agenda necessarily calls for less formal methodologies – approaches that are more institutional and historical in nature, and more interpretive in tone. How else could research accommodate the school's wider range of analytical concerns?

A more open range plainly is antithetical to the sort of reduction-ist epistemology favored by the American school. Methods should be eclectic, freed from the constraints of a hard science model. The search for firm evidence should not be allowed to stand in the way of the Big Picture. Breadth of vision should not to be sacrificed on the alter of strict social-science conventions as understood in the United States. The preference was captured well by a British-school friend of mine who said one day: "I don't do findings. I do interpretation."

Eclecticism does not necessarily mean a relaxation of scholarly stand-ards. Rejection of demanding hypothetico-deductivism need not imply abandonment of analytical rigor. In fact, British scholars are, on the whole, every bit as committed to the careful use of theory as are their American counterparts. Nor do more informal methodologies neces-sarily mean a contempt for empiricism, as Angus Cameron and Ronen Palan (2009) remind us. British scholars may eschew the sophisticated statistical techniques favored by the US mainstream, but they too understand the value of accurate observation and a close reading of real-world experience.

Nonetheless, as compared with the demanding standards employed by the American school, British methods clearly do leave something to be desired. Obscurity in the specification of empirical relationships is by no means a virtue. The British school's more relaxed approach to theory-building makes its efforts at generalization suspect. Its avoid-ance of quantitative data collection raises questions of stochastic valid-ity. And its disdain for formal testing hinders replicability. Here again we end up with a debilitating lack of focus.

Complementarity

None of this is meant to suggest that one of the two sides of the trans-atlantic divide is somehow "better" or "worse" than the other. Any such comparison would obviously be invidious. Neither camp deserves to be described as "vulgar" or "fraudulent." Rather, the relationship between the two factions is more akin to Akira Kurosawa's 1950 film *Rashomon*, where the same basic story was recalled in vastly different ways by separate narrators. Here the American school tells the story one way; the British school, another. Despite what many on either side of the Atlantic might contend, neither is inherently superior – quite the contrary, in fact.

In practice, the two schools complement each other neatly, the strengths of one largely balancing weaknesses of the other. The American side may take justifiable pride in its allegiance to the demanding principles of positivism and empiricism, but arguably it may also be reproached for its narrow preoccupation with scientific method and its disdain for normative work. Scholars working in the US style, absorbed with mid-level theory building, are frequently insular in their intellectual interests and indifferent to matters of equity or justice. Bold new ideas tend to be discouraged by the need to demonstrate careful methodological rigor. History and social context take a back seat to the parsimony of abstract, deductive logic.

Scholars on the British side, in contrast, help to compensate for such shortcomings with their intellectual ecumenism and their skeptical attitude toward orthodoxy. The British style may be fairly criticized for its less systematic approach to theory-building and testing, which makes generalization difficult and cumulation of knowledge virtually impossible. However, Britain's scholars may also legitimately claim to make a useful contribution by opening discourse to the insights of a wider range of disciplines and by highlighting the normative element in scholarly inquiry. The more open range for research permits consideration of grander historical narratives. Each school adds value in its own way. Advanced students of IPE can learn much from both.

We are reminded of the old adage explaining the difference between a specialist and a generalist. A specialist, it is said, is someone who learns more and more about less and less until she knows everything about nothing. A generalist, conversely, learns less and less about more and more until she knows nothing about everything. Both schools could benefit from keeping that bit of wisdom in mind.

References

Belfrage, Claes and Owen Worth (eds) (2012), "Special issue: critical international political economy – renewing critique and ontologies," *International Politics*, **49** (2), 131–135.

Blyth, Mark (2011), "Torn between two lovers? Caught in the middle of British and American IPE," in Nicola Phillips and Catherine E. Weaver (eds), *International Political Economy: Debating the Past, Present and Future*, London: Routledge, pp. 133–140.

Burnham, Peter (1994), "Open Marxism and vulgar international political economy," *Review of International Political Economy*, **1** (2), 221–231.

Cameron, Angus and Ronen Palan (2009), "Empiricism and objectivity: reflexive theory construction in a complex world," in Mark Blyth (ed.), *Routledge Handbook of International Political Economy (IPE): IPE as a Global Conversation*, London: Routledge, pp. 112–125.

Clift, Ben and Ben Rosamond (2009), "Lineages of a British international political economy," in Mark Blyth (ed.), *Routledge Handbook of International Political Economy (IPE): IPE as a Global Conversation*, London: Routledge, pp. 95–111.

Cohen, Benjamin J. (2007), "The transatlantic divide: why are American and British IPE so different?," *Review of International Political Economy*, **14** (2), 197–219.

Cox, Robert W. (1981), "Social forces, states and world orders: beyond international relations theory," *Millennium*, **10** (2), 126–155.

Cox, Robert W. (1987), *Production, Power, and World Order: Social Forces in the Making of History*, New York: Columbia University Press.

Cox, Robert W. (1999), "Conversation," *New Political Economy*, **4** (3), 389–398.

Dickins, Amanda (2006), "The evolution of international political economy," *International Affairs*, **82** (3), 479–492.

Gill, Stephen and David Law (1989), "Global hegemony and the structural power of capital," *International Studies Quarterly*, **33** (4), 475–499.

Gills, Barry K. (2001), "Re-orienting the new (international) political economy," *New Political Economy*, **6** (2), 233–245.

Griffiths, Martin (1999), *Fifty Key Thinkers in International Relations*, New York: Routledge.

Krätke, Michael R. and Geoffrey R.D. Underhill (2006), "Political economy: the revival of an interdiscipline,'" in Richard Stubbs and Geoffrey R.D. Underhill (eds), *Political Economy and the Changing Global Order*, third edition, New York: Oxford University Press, pp. 24–38.

Langley, Paul (2009), "Power–knowledge estranged: from Susan Strange to poststructuralism in British IPE," in Mark Blyth (ed.), *Routledge Handbook of International Political Economy (IPE): IPE as a Global Conversation*, London: Routledge, pp. 126–139.

Murphy, Craig N. and Douglas R. Nelson (2001), "International political economy: a tale of two heterodoxies," *British Journal of Politics and International Relations*, **3** (3), 393–412.

Murphy, Craig N. and Roger Tooze (1991), "Getting beyond the 'common sense' of the IPE orthodoxy," in Craig N. Murphy and Roger Tooze (eds), *The New International Political Economy*, Boulder, CO: Lynne Rienner, pp. 11–31.

O'Brien, Robert (1995), "International political economy and international relations: apprentice or teacher?," in John MacMillan and Andrew Linklater (eds), *Boundaries in Question: New Directions in International Relations*, London: Pinter, pp. 89–106.

O'Brien, Robert and Marc Williams (2010), *Global Political Economy*, third edition, London: Palgrave Macmillan.

Palan, Ronen P. (2000), "New trends in global political economy," in Ronen P. Palan (ed.), *Global Political Economy: Contemporary Theories*, London: Routledge, pp. 1–18.

Palan, Ronen P. and Barry Gills (eds) (1994), *Transcending the State–Global Divide: a Neostructuralist Agenda in International Relations*, Boulder, CO: Lynne Rienner.

Phillips, Nicola (2005), "'Globalizing' the study of international political economy," in Nicola Phillips (ed.), *Globalizing International Political Economy*, New York: Palgrave Macmillan, pp. 1–19.

Polanyi, Karl (1944), *The Great Transformation: The Political and Economic Origins of Our Time*, Boston, MA: Beacon Press.

Sharman, Jason C. and Catherine Weaver (2013), "RIPE, the American school, and diversity in global IPE," *Review of International Political Economy*, **20** (5), in press.

Shields, Stuart, Ian Bruff and Huw Macartney (eds) (2011), *Critical International Political Economy: Dialogue, Debate and Dissensus*, London: Palgrave Macmillan.

Strange, Susan (1970), "International economics and international relations: a case of mutual neglect," *International Affairs*, **46** (2), 304–315.

Strange, Susan (1984), "Preface," in Susan Strange (ed.), *Paths to International Political Economy*, London: George Allen & Unwin, ix–xi.

Strange, Susan (1988), Review of *Production, Power, and World Order*, by Robert Cox, *International Affairs*, **64** (2), 269–270.

Strange, Susan (1991), "An eclectic approach," in Craig N. Murphy and Roger Tooze (eds), *The New International Political Economy*, Boulder, CO: Lynne Rienner, pp. 33–49.

Strange, Susan (1994), Wake up, Krasner! The world *has* changed, *Review of International Political Economy*, **1** (2), 209–219.

Strange, Susan (1995), "ISA as a microcosm," *International Studies Quarterly*, **39** (3), 289–296.

Tooze, Roger, and Christopher May (2002), *Authority and Markets: Susan Strange's Writings on International Political Economy*, Basingstoke: Palgrave Macmillan.

Underhill, Geoffrey R.D. (2000), "State, market, and global political economy: genealogy of an (inter)discipline," *International Affairs*, **76** (4), 805–824.

Van Apeldoorn, Bastiaan, Ian Bruff and Magnus Ryner (2011), "The richness and diversity of critical IPE perspectives," in Nicola Phillips and Catherine E. Weaver (eds), *International Political Economy: Debating the Past, Present and Future*, London: Routledge, pp. 215–222.

Watson, Matthew (2005), *Foundations of International Political Economy*, New York: Palgrave Macmillan.

Weaver, Catherine (2011), "IPE's split brain," in Nicola Phillips and Catherine E. Weaver (eds), *International Political Economy: Debating the Past, Present and Future*, London: Routledge, pp. 141–149.

5 Britain's "Far-Out"

Just as the American school has its Left-Out, the British school has what we may jokingly call its "Far-Out" – distant parts of the former empire, far across the globe, where IPE has also taken root as a recognized field of study. Most prominent among the Far-Out are the one-time dominions of Australia and Canada, two nations each big enough to produce a "critical mass" of fresh candidates for the invisible college. In each case, interest in IPE was stimulated by the pioneering developments in the United States and Britain that first emerged in the 1970s. After a slow start, new cohorts began to coalesce in the 1980s that by now have grown sizable enough to make a mark in the world. Evidence suggests that, between them, Australia and Canada now host as much as 10 percent of the global invisible college (Sharman and Weaver 2013).

In each of the two countries, enough years have now passed for practices of intellectual reproduction to begin to shape distinctive discourse coalitions. In neither place, however, has the process yet gone so far as to produce anything that might be labeled a separate "school." In many ways both former dominions are still heavily influenced by intellectual fashions imported from Britain, the old mother country. This is especially true of Australia, where in the words of one younger Australian scholar (in private correspondence), "IPE is incredibly Anglophile." If it is less true of Canada, it is mainly because of that country's close proximity to the United States, which has the effect of diluting, somewhat, Britain's historical impact.

Australia

At first glance, Australian IPE's attachment to Britain might seem surprising, given the great physical distance between the two countries. Even in the age of the internet, face-to-face contact matters in scholarly discourse. Inside Australia – a nation long known as the Lucky

Country – specialists have been busy building an informal IPE network, with frequent meetings and workshops. Dialogue is vigorous. Active communication is much more difficult when your interlocutors are half-way around the globe, fast asleep during your peak working hours.

Yet the British influence has persisted ever since IPE first got started in the Lucky Country in the late 1980s. In good part that was because of institutional replication. As Jason Sharman, an emerging star of Australian IPE, has written: "Academia in Australia was founded on British lines, and remains within this mold in terms of its institutions, graduate training, and nomenclature" (Sharman 2009: 216). All that puts a limit on whatever influence might otherwise come from the United States. The effect is reinforced by established practices of intellectual reproduction. Continues Sharman, "Many more of those working in IPE in Australia have been trained in the UK than in the US, and certainly international career paths are much more likely to involve movement between Australia and Europe rather than Australia and the United States" (Sharman 2009: 219). Australian specialists also publish much more of their research in British journals than in US venues. In most respects, therefore, Australia's version of the field closely mimics its British counterpart. The main distinguishing feature of Australian IPE is its agenda which, understandably, has always been most heavily weighted toward Australia itself and relations with the Asian region, including most notably China.

The British connection

Australia's British connection is highly visible. Consider, for example, the role of John Ravenhill, long seen as one of the Lucky Country's leading scholars of IPE. Ravenhill's influence as a pioneer of the field in Australia rivals that of figures like Keohane and Gilpin in the United States or Strange and Cox in Britain. His origins, however, are British, as noted in Chapter 1, and his graduate training was in the United States and Canada. A classic transplant, he has held academic positions in Britain, moving back and forth between the home country and Australia before relocating recently to Canada. Among his most notable contributions to the development of the field in Australia is an edited anthology, *Global Political Economy*, widely used in the Lucky Country's universities and now in its fourth edition (Ravenhill 2014a). Of the volume's 14 contributors, only two are located in the United States. The rest, apart from one Swiss, are from Britain or Canada.

The influence of the British style is immediately evident in the choice of title for the anthology: *Global* (not *International*) *Political Economy*. As noted in the previous chapter, many British scholars promote the idea of calling their subject Global Political Economy in order to highlight their preference for a broader all-encompassing perspective. Ravenhill's choice of title clearly signals that, in line with Susan Strange's dictum, IR is to be considered a subdiscipline of the field (whether called IPE or GPE) and not the other way around. Nearly half the essays in the volume are on the subject of globalization, which the authors clearly take seriously.

Even more pointedly, Ravenhill preemptively defines the central focus of IPE as "the interrelationship between public and private power in the allocation of scarce resources" (Ravenhill 2014b: x). That slant on the field obviously contrasts sharply with the state-centric ontology of the American school. Likewise, Ravenhill declares that two of the most fundamental concerns of IPE are questions of distribution and power, neither of which feature prominently in the less normative US version of the field. He also celebrates a British-style emphasis on inclusiveness – an "open range" – as critical to the subject. "The study of global political economy," he writes, "has been enriched by the application of a diverse array of theoretical and methodological approaches" (Ravenhill 2014b: x). Strange could not have put it better. Nothing could be further from the American school's narrow preoccupation with the OEP paradigm and the conformity of "normal" science.

Nor is the Ravenhill volume in any way exceptional. Equally representative is a recent *Handbook on International Political Economy* (Pettman 2012a), another anthology intended for the Australian academic market. Among its two dozen chapters, almost all written by Australians, there is barely any mention at all of scholarship in the mainstream US tradition. When research outside Australia is cited, it is overwhelmingly from the British school or its first cousins in America's Left-Out. That is no accident, according to the volume's editor. Quite explicitly, the aim of the book is to give voice to "those marginalized by mainstream IPE," which presumably means the American school (Pettman 2012b: 14). In a foreword, Ravenhill (2012: vi) praises the collection as an effective antidote to "the depressing narrowness of much of the contemporary study of IPE." Who but the US mainstream could he possibly have in mind?

Rejection of US "narrowness" does not mean a relaxation of intellectual standards, any more than it does in the British school. Like their British

counterparts, Ravenhill and most of his Australian colleagues acknowl-
edge the value of positivist analysis and a commitment to accurate
observation. However, it does mean a distaste for the American school's
insistence on the virtues of strict hypothetico-deductivism, with all its
costs in terms of descriptive reality or credibility. In Australian IPE,
the US penchant for abstract reductionist models is seen as something
akin to the call of the sirens leading scholars astray, away from the rich
detail of history and social context. Australians must not be tempted
to travel the "high road" of technically sophisticated econometrics.
Preference, rather, is to be given to a broader organic comprehension
of society, as it is in the British school. "Substantivism" is the label
suggested by Richard Leaver, one of the Lucky Country's earliest IPE
experts. In Leaver's words: "Substantivism, by contrast, defines a low
road where emphasis falls upon the social and historical context . . .
The low road will define the one and only route to survival" (Leaver
2010: 126).

Like the British school, therefore, Australian IPE tends to be multidisciplinary, institutional, and historical. Inspiration comes from a variety
of related disciplines, including sociology, development studies, and
social theory. Typically, Australian IPE is also openly normative, again
in the tradition of classical political economy. Above all it is qualitative
and interpretive in tone. As Sharman comments:

> Most strikingly perhaps for an outside observer is the scarcity of quan-
> titative, rational choice, and formal modeling work . . . While qualitative
> methods, constructivism, and critical approaches may be an embattled
> and marginalized minority in the United States, jointly they are dominant
> (hegemonic, one might say) in Australia . . . Intellectual currents do not
> favor the taste for econometrics or micro-economic techniques that have
> come to characterize the field in the United States. (Sharman 2009: 219,
> 226)

Agenda

What, then, do Australians write about? What is their agenda? Under
the broad rubric of substantivism, topics vary considerably according
to the taste of individual scholars. In this respect, scholarship is eclectic. Trade and finance, historically the core concerns of IPE, naturally
attract much attention. Ravenhill, for instance, has written extensively
on trade regionalism, particularly in Australia's Asian neighborhood
(for example, Ravenhill 2001), while monetary relations have been the

focus of younger scholars like Leonard Seabrooke (2006) and Susan Park (2005). However, other diverse subjects come up as well, just as they do elsewhere. Environmental challenges, for example, have been explored by Charlotte Epstein (2008), while Penny Griffin (2007) has promoted the role of feminist theory in IPE. In addition, of course, the subject of globalization has come in for much discussion, most notably by Linda Weiss in a highly regarded treatise on *The Myth of the Powerless State* (1998).

However, given the small size of the Australian IPE community – by most counts, no more than 30–40 specialists in all – the scope of scholarship is, not surprisingly, rather more narrow than it is in the British or American schools. Australia has nothing like the traffic jam of competing research programs that we see in Britain, nor is there so much interest in the evolution of broader historical structures, whether called world-systems or world orders. In Australian IPE's one significant departure from the British model, analysis has for the most part remained largely state-centric, retaining the "shackles of meth-odological nationalism," and the most important state for Australian scholars has been, quite understandably, their own. Above all, atten-tion has traditionally focused on Australian foreign economic policy and the Asia-Pacific region. The objective for most has been to define the Lucky Country's national interests in the local and world econo-mies, with a particular emphasis on regional development and multi-lateral institutions. One source (Seabrooke and Elias 2010) describes this as an "institutionalist" perspective – an orientation, largely local and policy-driven, that is by far the most distinctive feature of the field in the Lucky Country. Although it would be unfair to accuse Australian IPE of outright parochialism, it would not be inaccurate to describe it as more than a little insular.

To a large extent, the community's degree of insularity would seem to reflect Australia's relative isolation at the far fringes of the Antipodes, which naturally concentrates the mind on local issues. For some, most notably Richard Higgott (1990), this peripheral position is a virtue, offering the basis for a distinctively "Antipodean IPE" that would focus on the role of middle-level powers like Australia in the global system. Few Australian scholars, however, have chosen to follow that particular path.

Insularity also appears to derive from the fact that, when IPE got its start in the Lucky Country, the field was seen largely as an offshoot of comparative political economy and development studies – quite different from the American school, with its origins in the international relations subdiscipline of political science; and from the British school, with its roots in international studies. The First Generation of Australian scholars – pioneers like Ravenhill, Higgott, Leaver, and Weiss – could be forgiven for a greater preoccupation with their own nation and its neighbors.

A comparative policy orientation was established early in a landmark study by Frank Castles on *Australian Public Policy and Economic Vulnerability* (1988). It has also long been evident in the contributions of Weiss, who has always been best known for her work on the politics of economic development. Even in *The Myth of the Powerless State* (1998), her primary interest was in domestic institutions and capabilities. Much of her later work has remained focused largely on local policy issues (Weiss *et al.* 2004). Likewise, a regional orientation was evident in one of the early landmark accomplishments of Australian IPE, a collection of essays on *Pacific Economic Relations in the 1990s* (Higgott *et al.* 1993). Ravenhill, together with colleagues, continues to address Asian regional issues (MacIntyre *et al.* 2008), as do others of his generation such as Higgott (2006).

Yet, increasingly, exceptions can be found, particularly among what may be considered Australia's rising Second Generation. In more recent years, a scattering of younger scholars has begun to move away from policy-driven research toward what one source (Seabrooke and Elias 2010) characterizes as a "sociological turn" in Australian IPE. Emphasis is placed less on defining national interests in the Asian region. Attention, instead, is directed more toward trends in the world economy that can be studied by examining smaller social environments, such as the internal bureaucracy of international organizations or the operations of various kinds of private transnational groups. A recent survey describes this is a shift "from multilateralism to microcosms," where the spotlight is on change within communities or institutions rather than in wider regional or global settings (Seabrooke and Elias 2010). Perhaps the most outstanding examples of such work to date have come from Sharman (2006, 2011), who has burrowed deeply into the role of tax havens and money laundering practices in the global economy.

For the sociological turn, however, it is still early days. Overall, the regional orientation of Australian IPE remains dominant and the community's main claim to distinction. Ravenhill (2009) is undoubtedly correct when he claims that the most notable contributions from Australian IPE scholars to date have been their studies of East Asia. Otherwise, the Lucky Country continues to rely most heavily on its British connection, little more than a distant Far-Out echo of an intellectual style born in Britain.

Canada

The story in Canada is different. In the 1980s, when IPE first began to take shape in that country, it largely centered on one man: Robert Cox. After more than a quarter-century of public service with the International Labour Organization in Geneva and then several years of teaching in the United States, Cox returned to his homeland in 1978 to take up a faculty position at York University in Toronto. With the publication of his breakthrough work in the 1980s (described in Chapter 4), he came to personify the newborn field of IPE in Canada. York University, one Canadian has written, soon was able "to claim for itself the mantle of Canada's *national* school of IPE" (Germain 2009: 80), with Cox as its avatar – a kind of one-man First Generation. Such was his influence that some claimed that a distinct Canadian school of IPE, inspired by Cox, had emerged to rival those in the United States and Britain (Chavagneux 2010).

Over time, however, as a Second Generation of scholars has come along, the picture has grown more complex, defying such easy categorization. To begin, Canada is a bilingual country, with some scholars working in the French language rather than English. Although to date IPE has not progressed very far in the Francophone branch of Canadian academia, based in the province of Quebec, a limited amount of scholarship has begun to appear, not surprisingly influenced in particular by debates in French universities. However, little of that work has made any impact on the much larger Anglophone branch of Canadian academia, where development of the field is significantly more advanced – but also more divided. Even among English speakers today, there is no such thing as a single Canadian school.

In fact, IPE in Anglophone Canada has become deeply fractured, too diverse to characterize in any monolithic fashion. Canadians themselves use words like variety, heterogeneity, even disorganized, to characterize the present state of their field. One might say that there are many Canadian schools of IPE. As one senior scholar wrote to me in private correspondence, in Canada "there are identifiable clusters around particular theoretical approaches, methods or issue areas, but they do not have a brand that brings them together." In effect Canadians, in their one country, accurately reflect the striking diversity of the field that prevails across the globe more broadly.

Dominating the picture is a cleavage between British and American influences – the transatlantic divide in miniature. On the one side, as in Australia, the British connection lingers, still a strong part of Anglophone Canada's sense of identity. The impact of the British style of IPE is widespread, not least because of Cox's role in providing the British school's foundational model. However, on the other side there is also an unavoidable American connection, stemming from the hard facts of geography. The Americans, like it or not, are just next door, sharing a common language and the world's longest border. To paraphrase Porfirio Diaz's lament about Mexico, we might say: poor Canada, so far from the mother country, so close to the United States. Many Canadians cannot help but be attracted by the siren call of the American style of IPE. Says Randall Germain (2009: 84), an astute observer, these competing influences put Canadian IPE "at the crossroads of transatlantic scholarly exchange."

The British connection

The strength of the British connection, as in Australia, owes much to institutional replication. In Canada too, academia was founded on British lines and, for the most part, continues to be structured like Britain's university system; many Canadians still get their training in Britain; and many Britons teach in Canada. However, much is also owed to the lasting impact of Cox, who remained professionally active even after his formal retirement in 1996. Many of his papers have been collected together in two influential edited volumes (Cox and Sinclair 1996; Cox and Schechter 2002). Much of his ongoing effort went into refining his concept of the "state–society complex," which he later described as "a *nébuleuse* personified as the global economy . . . a transnational process of consensus formation among the official care-takers of the global economy" (Cox and Sinclair 1996: 298, 301). The *nébuleuse*, in turn, was redefined by Geoffrey Underhill, a Canadian trained at Oxford University, as a "state–market condominium" – an "integrated system [that] operates simultaneously through the competitive pressures of the market and the political processes which shape the boundaries and structures within which that competition (or lack thereof) takes place" (Underhill 2000: 808). In homage to Cox, Underhill describes the study of Cox's state–society complex as "*the* problem of international political economy" (Underhill 2006: 16).

For many in Canada, Cox's ideas remain paramount. IPE, it is felt, is best understood in non-reductionist historical materialist terms; it should be multidisciplinary in nature and normative in tone. The core problematique is ecumenical, as it is in the British school (as well as among the British school's first cousins, America's Left-Out). Research should encompass a broad range of social and ethical questions. Theory should aim to be critical, not "problem-solving." Attention should be directed to the implications of broad systemic transformation for such vital life issues as inequality, class formation, and economic development. The goal, ultimately, should be to replace capitalism "with something nicer."

Not surprisingly, all this continues to be the hallmark of scholarship at York University, where Cox's world orders approach lives on. This is particularly evident in the work of his younger colleague Stephen Gill, a Briton by birth who was recruited by York in 1991. As early as 1989, in an influential paper written with David Law (Gill and Law 1989), Gill explicitly built on Cox's dynamics to explain what he described as the structural power of capitalism. In a long parade of subsequent publications, he has continued to add insights to Cox's foundational framework, introducing allied concepts like "market civilization" and "new constitutionalism" (Gill 2003). Market civilization stands for the way in which market forces and values have, in Gill's view, become increasingly pervasive, working their way into the very micro-practices of everyday life. New constitutionalism refers to an emerging governance framework that empowers the disciplines of the marketplace to reshape economic and social development worldwide. Also active at York are Isabella Bakker, a radical feminist scholar (Bakker 2007), and Leo Panitch, a long-time exponent of Marxist interpretations of global economic history (Panitch and Gindin 2012). To this day, York University remains a center for studies in the tradition of historical materialism and critical theory.

However, by now Cox's influence has spread elsewhere as well – not least because of the generations of students from York who have fanned out to take up positions at other Canadian universities (as well as in Britain and elsewhere). Across Canada's landscape today we find many scholars inspired by the same broadly historical frame-work. A few work primarily in the French language, such as Hélène Pellerin, an expert on international migration, and André Drainville, who writes about globalization. Most, however, are part of the larger Anglophone community. One prominent example is Claire Cutler (2003), who uses critical theory to explore legal dimensions of the world economy. Others include Randall Germain (1997), Tony Porter (2005), and Susanne Soederberg (2004), all inspired by Cox's ideas in their efforts to explore the development of governance arrangements in global finance. All tend to publish much of their work in Britain, where they find a more congenial audience than in the United States, and many maintain ties with British universities. For them, the British connection endures.

The American connection

Also enduring is an American connection, nourished by geographic proximity and a parallel form of institutional replication. For an increasing number of Canadian scholars, ties now run primarily across the border to the United States rather than across the pond to Britain. Many have studied in the United States or have taught there. Canadians cannot help but notice the emergence of a dominant model to their south, with all its claims to maturity and normalization. It is easy to believe that the OEP paradigm does indeed set the standard for professionalism in the field. Hence it is easy to be seduced by the tech-nical sophistication of a hard science methodology. Canadians cannot be blamed for aspiring to respect too.

As in the United States, accordingly, there is much interest in the state-centric ontology of the American school, with its focus on ques-tions of state behavior and system governance. However, also as in the United States, there is much within-type variance, replicating the broad debates that have dominated mainstream US scholarship over the years.

The liberal tradition, for example, was long represented by Mark Zacher, one of the original contributors to the landmark volume on *International Regimes* published back in 1983 (Finlayson and Zacher 1983). Until his recent retirement, Zacher consistently employed neo-liberal themes to examine institutional developments in international economic management. Likewise, the influence of the realist tradition has long been evident in the work of scholars like Michael Webb and

Mark Brawley, both of whom were trained in the United States. Webb (1995) has explored the difficulties of promoting monetary coopera-tion among sovereign, self-interested governments. Brawley (1993, 1999) has provided much insight into the nature of hegemonic lead-ership in the international system. The theme of hegemony has also been taken up more recently by Carla Norrlof (2010) in an insightful analysis of the reasons for the durability of US leadership in the world economy. Constructivism too has arrived to animate the research of a number of younger scholars – most notably Jacqueline Best (2005) in an intriguing study of the role that ambiguity plays in international monetary governance.

Building bridges?

Given the conflicting pressures of the British and American connec-tions, at the crossroads of the transatlantic divide, it is certainly not surprising that we might find vocal proponents of each style in Canada. What is perhaps more unexpected is the number of scholars who prefer to keep a foot in each camp, respecting the American school's emphasis on scientific positivism and empiricism even while heark-ening to the attractions of British-style historicism and inclusiveness – seeking, in effect, to build bridges between the two traditions. A Canadian friend once described the approach to me as "engaged eclec-ticism." I was reminded of the laugh line attributed to a well-known American baseball player, Yogi Berra, who is supposed to have said: "When you arrive at a fork in the road, take it!"

Perhaps most prominent among these "bridge builders" is Eric Helleiner, regarded as among the top IPE scholars in Canada today. Ever since his first book on the post-World War II global monetary system, published in 1994 (Helleiner 1994), Helleiner has shown an exceptional skill at blending meticulous empirical observation and the-oretically informed analysis with an acute appreciation of the roles of history, institutions, and ideas. In the decades since that book's appear-ance, his research has addressed a remarkably wide range of issues, from the origins of money (2003) to the enduring role of national economic culture (Helleiner and Pickel 2005).

Another especially important bridge builder is Louis Pauly, an American based in Canada, who has written extensively on issues of international finance (1988, 1997), among other subjects. Behind the scenes, during a five-year stint as co-editor of the influential journal

International Organization, he worked hard to encourage scholarship that combined the best of the American and British styles. A third key figure is Jennifer Clapp, with path-breaking books on environmental and food issues (2001, 2012).

If there is anyone who may be said to represent a truly distinctive Canadian IPE, it is scholars like these, with their unusual degree of pragmatism. Some Canadians speak of their intellectual pluralism; others use words like openness or elasticity. Nothing better illustrates the germ of truth in the old cliché about Canadian moderation. (Question: Why does a Canadian cross the road? Answer: To get to the middle.) The invisible college could use more such moderates to help facilitate communication between the field's often insular factions.

References

Bakker, Isabella (2007), "Social reproduction and the constitution of a gendered political economy," *New Political Economy,* **12** (4), 541–556.

Best, Jacqueline (2005), *The Limits of Transparency: Ambiguity and the History of International Finance,* Ithaca, NY: Cornell University Press.

Brawley, Mark (1993), *Liberal Leadership,* Ithaca, NY: Cornell University Press.

Brawley, Mark (1999), *Afterglow or Adjustment?,* New York: Columbia University Press.

Castles, Francis G. (1988), *Australian Public Policy and Economic Vulnerability,* Sydney: Allen and Unwin.

Chavagneux, Christian (2010), *Économie Politique Internationale,* second edition, Paris: Editions La Découverte. [First edition published in 2004.]

Clapp, Jennifer (2001), *Toxic Exports: The Transfer of Hazardous Wastes from Rich to Poor Countries,* Ithaca, NY: Cornell University Press.

Clapp, Jennifer (2012), *Hunger in the Balance: The New Politics of International Food Aid,* Ithaca, NY: Cornell University Press.

Cox, Robert W. (1996), "Global *perestroika,*" in Robert W. Cox with Timothy J. Sinclair, *Approaches to World Order,* New York: Cambridge University Press, pp. 296–313.

Cox, Robert W. with Michael G. Schechter (2002), *The Political Economy of a Plural World: Critical Reflections on Power, Morals, and Civilization,* New York: Routledge.

Cox, Robert W. with Timothy J. Sinclair (1996), *Approaches to World Order,* New York: Cambridge University Press.

Cutler, A. Claire (2003), *Private Power and Global Authority: Transnational Merchant Law in the Global Political Economy,* New York: Cambridge University Press.

Epstein, Charlotte (2008), *Producing Whales, Performing Power: A Study of Discourse in International Relations,* Cambridge, MA: MIT Press.

Finlayson, Jock A. and Mark W. Zacher (1983), "The GATT and the regulation of trade barriers: regime dynamics and functions," in Stephen D. Krasner (ed.), *International Regimes,* Ithaca, NY: Cornell University Press.

Germain, Randall D. (1997), *The International Organization of Credit: States and Global Finance in the World-Economy*, New York: Cambridge University Press.

Germain, Randall D. (2009), "Of margins, traditions, and engagements: a brief disciplinary history of IPE in Canada," in Mark Blyth (ed.), *Routledge Handbook of International Political Economy (IPE): IPE as a Global Conversation*, London: Routledge, pp. 77–91.

Gill, Stephen (2003), *Power and Resistance in the New World Order*, London: Palgrave Macmillan.

Gill, Stephen and David Law (1989), "Global hegemony and the structural power of capitalism," *International Studies Quarterly*, **33** (4), 475–499.

Griffin, Penny (2007), "Refashioning IPE: what and how gender analysis teaches international (global) political economy," *Review of International Political Economy*, **14** (4), 719–736.

Helleiner, Eric N. (1994), *States and the Reemergence of Global Finance: From Bretton Woods to the 1990s*, Ithaca, NY: Cornell University Press.

Helleiner, Eric N. and Andreas Pickel (eds) (2005), *Economic Nationalism in a Globalizing World*, Ithaca, NY: Cornell University Press.

Higgott, Richard A. (1990), "Toward a non-hegemonic IPE: an Antipodean perspective," Working Paper 97, Canberra: Peace Research Centre, Australian National University.

Higgott, Richard A. (2006), "Economic regionalism in East Asia: consolidation with centrifugal tendencies," in Richard Stubbs and Geoffrey R.D. Underhill (eds), *Political Economy and the Changing Global Order*, third edition, Oxford: Oxford University Press, pp. 344–355.

Higgott, Richard A., Richard Leaver and John Ravenhill (eds) (1993), *Pacific Economic Relations in the 1990s: Conflict or Cooperation?*, Sydney: Allen and Unwin.

Leaver, Richard (2010), "An Australian international political economy? The high road and the low road," *Australian Journal of International Affairs*, **64** (1), 123–129.

MacIntyre, Andrew, T.J. Pempel and John Ravenhill (eds) (2008), *Crisis as Catalyst: Asia's Dynamic Political Economy*, Ithaca, NY: Cornell University Press.

Norrlof, Carla (2010), *America's Global Advantage: US Hegemony and International Cooperation*, New York: Cambridge University Press.

Panitch, Leo and Sam Gindin (2012), *The Making of Global Capitalism: The Political Economy of American Empire*, London: Verso.

Park, Susan (2005), "Norm diffusion within international organizations: a case study of the World Bank," *Journal of International Relations and Development*, **8** (2), 114–141.

Pauly, Louis W. (1988), *Opening Financial Markets: Banking Politics on the Pacific Rim*, Ithaca, NY: Cornell University Press.

Pauly, Louis W. (1997), *Who Elected the Bankers? Surveillance and Control in the World Economy*, Ithaca, NY: Cornell University Press.

Pettman, Ralph (ed.) (2012a), *Handbook on International Political Economy*, Singapore: World Scientific.

Pettman, Ralph (2012b), "International political economy: competing analyses," in Ralph Pettman (ed.), *Handbook on International Political Economy*, Singapore: World Scientific, pp. 3–17.

Porter, Tony (2005), *Globalization and Finance*, Malden, MA: Polity Press.

Ravenhill, John (2001), *APEC and the Construction of Pacific Rim Regionalism*, Cambridge: Cambridge University Press.

Ravenhill, John (2009), "East Asian regionalism: much ado about nothing?," *Review of International Studies*, **35** (S1), 215–235.

Ravenhill, John (2012), "Foreword," in Ralph Pettman (ed.) *Handbook on International Political Economy*, Singapore: World Scientific, v–vi.

Ravenhill, John (ed.) (2014a), *Global Political Economy*, fourth edition, Oxford: Oxford University Press.

Ravenhill, John (2014b), "The study of global political economy," in John Ravenhill (ed.), *Global Political Economy*, fourth edition, Oxford: Oxford University Press, in press.

Seabrooke, Leonard (2006), *The Social Sources of Financial Power: Domestic Legitimacy and International Financial Orders*, Ithaca, NY: Cornell University Press.

Seabrooke, Leonard and Juanita Elias (2010), "From multilateralism to microcosms in the world economy: the sociological turn in Australian international political economy scholarship," *Australian Journal of International Affairs*, **64** (1), 1–12.

Sharman, Jason C. (2006), *Havens in a Storm: The Struggle for Global Tax Regulation*, Ithaca, NY: Cornell University Press.

Sharman, Jason C. (2009), "Neither Asia nor America: IPE in Australia," in Mark Blyth (ed.), *Routledge Handbook of International Political Economy (IPE): IPE as a Global Conversation*, London: Routledge, pp. 216–227.

Sharman, Jason C. (2011), *The Money Laundry: Regulating Criminal Finance in the Global Economy*, Ithaca, NY: Cornell University Press.

Sharman, Jason C. and Catherine Weaver (2013), "RIPE, the American school, and diversity in global IPE," *Review of International Political Economy*, **20** (5), in press.

Soederberg, Susanne (2004), *The Politics of the New International Financial Architecture: Reimposing Neoliberal Domination in the Global South*, London: Zed.

Underhill, Geoffrey R.D. (2000), "State, market, and global political economy: genealogy of an (inter)discipline," *International Affairs*, **76** (4), 805–824.

Underhill, Geoffrey R.D. (2006), "Introduction: conceptualizing the changing global order," in Richard Stubbs and Geoffrey R.D. Underhill (eds), *Political Economy and the Changing Global Order*, third edition, New York: Oxford University Press, pp. 3–23.

Webb, Michael C. (1995), *The Political Economy of Policy Coordination: International Adjustment since 1945*, Ithaca, NY: Cornell University Press.

Weiss, Linda M. (1998), *The Myth of the Powerless State*, Ithaca, NY: Cornell University Press.

Weiss, Linda M., Elizabeth Thurbon and John A. Mathews (2004), *How to Kill a Country: Australia's Devastating Trade Deal with the United States*, Sydney: Allen and Unwin.

6   Continental Europe

"We are with Europe but not of it," Winston Churchill once said. The English Channel may be narrow enough to swim across, but in cultural as well as political terms the distance between Britain and its Continental neighbors has always been immense – certainly greater than the distance between Britain and its Far-Out. The British attitude was best summed up years ago by a notorious London newspaper headline: "Fog in Channel – Continent Isolated."

Nothing better illustrates the enormity of the gap than the contrast in the standing of IPE on either side of what the French call La Manche. On the British side the modern field is well established, with roots going back to the classical political economy of the eighteenth century, and by now well into its Third Generation. On the Continent, by contrast, the development of a distinct research community has scarcely even begun. Interest in the subject is clearly spreading; IPE in Europe may be considered a healthy growth area. Yet relatively few scholars, as yet, choose to define themselves as specialists in the field as such. Most have been trained in more institutionalized academic traditions, such as international relations, political science, economics or sociology, and that is how they continue to think of themselves. The overlap with comparative political economy is particularly evident. IPE as such is not yet treated widely as a separate, formal area of study in the way that it is in Britain or elsewhere in the Anglosphere. In that sense, Frenchman Nicolas Jabko (2009: 213) is not far off the mark when he laments that "the study of international political economy is almost absent in continental Europe."

In fact, IPE on the Continent today resembles nothing so much as an archipelago – a scattering of islands, small cohorts here or there struggling to gain a place for themselves in the greater invisible college. In many countries the field remains nascent, barely acknowledged as a proper focal point for inquiry. Surprisingly, these include some of the Continent's biggest states, such as France, Italy, and Spain. In only a handful of countries has a sufficient number of scholars as yet managed to come together to carve out a distinctive identity. These include, most notably, the Nordic states, Germany, Switzerland, and the Netherlands. Across Europe as a whole, there still appears to be little cohesion and certainly nothing that could yet be described as a single Continental school. Within-type variance is considerable. As a collectivity, Europe today punches below its weight in the global IPE conversation.

Barriers

Why has Europe so lagged behind? What are the barriers that have inhibited the development of a Continental version of IPE?

Language is clearly a large part of the problem. America and Britain may be two nations divided by a common language, as Churchill quipped – but at least they can talk to each other and read each other's scholarship. The same may be said of the Australians and Anglophone Canadians as well. The Continent, by contrast, is divided by myriad separate tongues, making any sort of dialogue difficult. Not many Spanish scholars are likely to read work published in Norwegian or Czech. Danes can be expected to have some difficulty with Portuguese or Greek. For any sort of conversation to proceed, Europeans must resort to a common second language. To the chagrin of many Francophones, Europe's lingua franca has turned out to be English (the first language in history to be spoken by more people as a second language than as a primary language). Those lacking proficiency in English are effectively barred from full participation. They are limited in their access to the vast literature that has been produced over several decades by the American and British schools. Worse, unless they write well in English, they are hampered in gaining wider dissemination for their own professional work. As one European ruefully notes, native English speakers "get an extra 'bonus' in the academic world because of the language factor" (Hveem 2011: 176).

The language barrier also makes it difficult to develop publishing venues – journals or book publishers – that can be commonly used by scholars across the Continent. Not even in a nation as big as Germany, with a population of 80 million, do there seem to be enough specialists to convince anyone to start a journal dedicated to the field. If German scholars want to publish something in their own language, they must use more generalist journals such as *Zeitschrift für Internationale Beziehungen* (an IR journal) or *Politische Vierteljahresschrift* (the flagship journal of the German Political Science Association). Continental Europeans who aspire to reach a sizable IPE audience are compelled to submit their work to Anglophone outlets – most often in Britain, less frequently in the United States. The only local journals of any note capable of bringing research in the field to a broader Continental audience are the *European Journal of Political Economy*, the *European Journal of International Relations*, and the *Journal of International Relations and Development*, all published in English. None specializes specifically in IPE.

Likewise, language is undoubtedly a major reason why Europeans have not yet been able to institutionalize a broad research network for the field comparable to the APSA and ISA sections in the United States or IPEG in Britain. Even America's Left-Out have their Political Economy of the World-System section in the American Sociological Association. *Faute de mieux*, most Continental scholars hoping to be part of IPE's invisible college join Britain's IPEG or America's ISA and attend their annual meetings. On occasion, attempts have been made to foster closer relations among specialists across the Continent. Perhaps most noteworthy was the European Political Economy Infrastructure Consortium (EPIC), an effort begun in 1999 to promote a loose network structure for European scholars through training programs, academic workshops, and a dedicated online journal, the *European Political Economy Review* (*EPER*). Although it enjoyed impressive backing, with support from key institutions in Britain, Germany, Italy, and Spain, EPIC lasted only three years before going out of existence. *EPER* died in 2009. Today the main forums available to scholars on the Continent are the Political Economy Section of the long-established European Consortium for Political Research (ECPR) and ECPR's newer offshoot, the European International Studies Association (EISA).

However, language is not the only problem. European IPE is divided as well by deeply entrenched differences of intellectual culture, which also hinder productive communication. Nations on the Continent have had literally centuries to develop their own distinctive norms and standards for scholarship, reinforced by generations of professional socialization. Contrasts between, say, French rationalism and German historicism may be easy to caricature but nonetheless contains a vital seed of truth. Even when they all speak English, European scholars have a hard time talking to one another, let alone collaborating in the cultivation of a common field of study.

Finally, there is the inflexible traditionalism of most Continental academic systems, which limits employment opportunities for scholars who aspire to specialize in IPE. Most universities are state institutions, slow to adapt to the development of new research fields. Few departments formally reserve faculty slots for IPE specialists, as is now routinely done in the Anglosphere. Even fewer universities have created teaching or research programs in the field. That helps to explain why, in so many places across Europe, IPE must rely on scholars with a base in more established academic traditions to gain even a toe-hold in the academic firmament. Illustrative is the most recent TRIP survey of the field of international relations (Maliniak *et al.* 2012), which included a handful of European countries. In Denmark, only 2 percent of researchers specified IPE as their main area of research, as compared with 20 percent who claimed it as a secondary interest. In Norway, the comparable figures were 12 and 21 percent. By contrast, the numbers in the United States and Britain for IPE as a primary interest were considerably higher and roughly equal to the share of scholars listing IPE as a secondary area (Maliniak *et al.* 2012: Tables 22 and 23).

One sad consequence of Europe's academic traditionalism is a sizable exodus of scholars to faculty appointments elsewhere where they feel their professional interests are more welcome. One example is Jabko, trained in an American university, who ultimately returned to the United States after years of frustration trying to promote the study of IPE in France. Another is Jan Nederveen Pieterse, a Dutch student of globalization with ties to both the British school and America's Left-Out, who now teaches in California. Still others have crossed the English Channel for positions in British universities. Continental IPE, unfortunately, suffers from something of a brain drain.

Islands

Given these barriers, it is hardly surprising that there is still no Continental version of IPE. Discourse coalitions have come together, but so far only on a smaller scale, with most confined to a single nation or group of contiguous states – as noted, like islands in an archipelago. Many of the islands, on their own, tend to display only a relatively modest degree of within-type variance. Between them, however, differences remain considerable, paralleling and in some instances adding to the rich diversity of styles to be found in the modern field of IPE across the globe.

Scandinavia

Among the earliest islands to emerge in the Continental archipelago was a movement in Scandinavia, starting with the path-breaking work of the Norwegian Helge Hveem. As early as the 1970s, Hveem was already thinking about the nature of the global political economy (Hveem 1973), and in 1996 he published the first IPE textbook to be written in a Scandinavian language (1996). Over his long career, he has moved from an initial interest in development issues and regionalism to broader questions about the role of knowledge and cognition in the governance of the world economy (Hveem and Knutsen 2012). From the start, his scholarship was more in line with the inclusive spirit of the British school. In his words, "I see variety and complexity in the subject matter we study and prefer pluralist, eclectic theorising to reductionist, single-cause theory" (Hveem 2011: 174). Hveem's broad perspective and normative leanings have set the tone for much of the work that has followed in the Nordic region.

Despite his seminal role, Hveem himself insists that "there is no 'Scandinavian school' in IPE" (Hveem 2011: 176). However, that may be a little too modest. Scandinavians do have a publishing venue of their own, the *Nordic Journal of Political Economy*, which has been in existence for nearly four decades. It is true that in its pages it is difficult to find any degree of consensus on anything like a common ontology. While many researchers are comfortable to work within a conventional state-centric paradigm, for others the basic unit of analysis may be as narrow as the individual or as broad as the global system. There are no signs of convergence on a single foundational model like OEP or world-systems theory. However, it is also true that there is a fair amount of concord on other matters, such as agenda. Not surprisingly, a large part of formal scholarship is concerned with issues close to home – the Nordic welfare state, European integration, and the global oil industry. (Norway is a major oil exporter.) Reflecting the region's traditional strength in conventional economics, much work is also devoted to economic policy questions, including especially economic development in poorer regions of the world. (Sweden is the home of the Nobel Prize in Economics.) Likewise, much research also is devoted to multilateral organizations and the challenge of global economic governance, reflecting the region's interest in peace studies. (Norway is home to the Nobel Peace Prize.)

Moreover, Scandinavian scholars seem to concur in seeing the purpose of research as normative, not just explanatory; and most, like Hveem, tend to be open to ideas and insights from a variety of related disciplines. Interestingly, there is also a fairly broad commitment to serious empirical analysis, including large-scale quantitative methodologies, which is more in the spirit of the American School. There are also systematic efforts to cultivate communication and cooperation among IPE scholars in the region, such as the IPE Øresund/Öresund network, grouping together six institutions in Denmark and Sweden, that was started in 2012. Overall, there may not be anything as coherent as a Scandinavian school as such, but there is certainly ample evidence of a separate faction of the invisible college with its own distinguishing characteristics.

Worth special mention is a cohort of scholars in Denmark, led by Leonard Seabrooke (transplanted from Australia), who have promoted an innovative approach to IPE that they label "Everyday IPE" – EIPE (Hobson and Seabrooke 2007, 2009). EIPE stands in contrast to more conventional approaches, which are collectively labeled "Regulatory IPE." The distinction is ontological. Who are the key actors for purposes of analysis? In more conventional approaches, according to Seabrooke and his colleagues, the answer is almost always some set of elite agents – hegemonic powers, international institutions, the capitalist class, and the like. The view is top-down, with a few above setting rules for the many below. With EIPE, by contrast, the view is bottom-up, focusing not on "power makers" – the regulators – but on everyday folk, society's diverse masses of "power takers." Through their routine daily practices and patterns of behavior, non-elite actors can confer or withhold legitimacy from elite dictates and thus exercise an independent influence on outcomes. It may be a bit premature to declare EIPE "a new and emergent school of IPE," as does one source (Blyth 2009: 18), but it is clear that the approach does offer a fresh and distinctive take on what the field of IPE is all about.

Germany

Next door, in the Federal Republic of Germany, interest in IPE has been spreading rapidly in recent years, in good part because of growing exposure to scholarship coming out of the United States and Britain.

Tangible evidence can be found in German academia where, in contrast to most other European countries, universities are increasingly opening up faculty positions for specialists in the field. However, German IPE is also quite fragmented, with different clusters of scholars building their research on very different intellectual foundations. For the moment, within-type variance in Germany is far greater than in the Nordic group.

One of the oldest intellectual traditions in Germany is, not surprisingly, Marxism, which still exercises a strong influence on a good portion of German scholarship, along with the old Frankfurt School of dissident Marxists and more contemporary critical theory. Representative of Germans working in this tradition today is Elmar Altvater, along with his partner Birgit Mahnkopf, two staunch critics of global capitalism. In a series of joint publications over the years (for example, Altvater and Mahnkopf 1996, 2007) the pair has promoted a radical agenda that would not seem unfamiliar to any member of America's Left-Out. Others include Hans-Jürgen Bieling, who works on issues of European integration, and Andreas Nölke, with interests in corporate governance regulation and the "financialization" of contemporary society. Like the heterodox Left-Out, German scholars working in the Marxist tradition often come from a background in sociology and share with the Left-Out, as well as with many in the British school, a determined normative bent. They too would wish to make the world a better place.

Closely related is another tradition of long-standing in Germany – historical institutionalism – which uses institutions to understand sequences of social, political, and economic behavior and their patterns of change over time. Complex institutional mechanisms determine how societies respond to unexpected policy challenges and cope with the dynamics and feedbacks of underlying causal processes. As in both world-systems theory and Cox's notion of world orders, the focus typically is on broad global structures and the perspective is long term. As in comparative political economy, structured case studies are the methodology of choice. The influence of this tradition can be found most notably at the Max Planck Institute for the Study of Societies, located in Cologne.

Yet others scholars draw their inspiration from more conventional approaches to comparative political economy. A leading example is Suzanne Lütz (2002), an authority on financial markets who started her career as a comparativist before moving on to more global applications.

In the Federal Republic, the first studies of globalization were framed by comparativists in terms of a challenge to the viability of the welfare state. Debates centered on the distributional implications of a shrinking welfare state and on how welfare systems might be adapted to better resist international pressures. More recently, attention has shifted to a growing literature on European political economy, focusing on issues of economic and political integration on the Continent.

Finally, there are those who in American fashion are influenced most by conventional IR theory, emphasizing rationalist approaches, interests, and institutions. Popular subjects include European integration, international trade, and global economic governance. Representative is a recent edited volume on *New Rules for Global Markets: Public and Private Governance in the World Economy* (Schirm 2004). With its essays on states and international organizations as actors in global economic governance, the volume would be regarded as utterly orthodox by members of the American school. This cadre can only be expected to grow as more and more Germans return to their country with degrees from US institutions, where OEP reigns.

In time, of course, many or all of these traditions may well begin to converge to create something that might be described as a genuinely German IPE (or perhaps even become a model for a truly Continental IPE). However, judging from the state of scholarship at the moment, that day may still be quite far off. Although some Germans already see signs of a budding consensus, emphasizing mutually endogenous linkages between domestic and international institutions and structures, for now the Federal Republic remains host to a plethora of styles with little in common.

Switzerland and the Netherlands

Other islands of note can be found in two of Germany's closest neighbors, Switzerland and the Netherlands – small countries with very open economies, where an interest in the political economy of international relations would seem only natural. Both are host to a fair amount of IPE scholarship. Debates are lively, even robust, but the styles of what is done in the two nations could hardly be more different.

In Switzerland two distinct traditions compete, echoing to some extent the kind of fragmentation that exists in Germany. On one side is a cluster of scholars whose research stresses above all critical theory and historical materialism, in a manner reminiscent of the British school. A leading example is Jean-Christophe Graz, coming out of a background at both Sussex University in Britain and York University in Canada. The approach of this group is strongly interdisciplinary, normative, and determinedly "nontraditional." Their agenda is well indicated by a now-annual series of conferences on "Critical Voices in Swiss International Relations," which have addressed such topics as global governance, post-colonial theory, and feminism. However, on the other side is a cohort that takes its inspiration more from the mainstream American school of IPE. Many – such as Cedric Dupont, editor of the *Swiss Political Science Review*, and Thomas Bernauer, who specializes in environmental issues – have spent time at US universities, absorbing the standards of the mainstream US version of the field. Their agenda is more conventional, with a particular emphasis on issues of European integration. As in the United States, the cleavage between the two Swiss camps is deep. They barely talk to each other.

In the Netherlands, by contrast, IPE is more homogenous and has moved much more in the direction of the British school. Back in the early 1980s an "Amsterdam school of international political economy" began to coalesce, with roots in traditional Marxist class analysis (Pistor 2005). Among its more notable contributors were Henk Overbeek (2008) and Kees van der Pijl (1984, 1998), but in more recent years the original Amsterdam school has been largely eclipsed by the emergence of a younger generation of scholars less wedded to the rigid dialectics of classical historical materialism. They prefer an agenda and style more like that of their peers across the English Channel; many even come from Britain or elsewhere. Perhaps best known is Geoffrey Underhill, the Oxford-trained Canadian, who for many years has taught at the University of Amsterdam. Most of Underhill's work is published in English, and with books like *States, Markets, and Governance* (2001) he has established himself as one of the leading proponents of the British style of IPE. A popular anthology that he has edited together with another Canadian, Richard Stubbs (Stubbs and Underhill 2006), is widely used in British universities. It is telling that the volume, now in its third edition, is dedicated to none other than Susan Strange. In effect, the Dutch island today can be considered a cross-channel outpost of the version of the field that Strange did so much to shape in her own country.

Elsewhere

Elsewhere on the Continent a scattering of other scholars can be found struggling to join the invisible college, but in numbers that are typically too miniscule to warrant separate discussion. In some countries, IPE has not even yet made an appearance. In others, efforts have been made to stir up interest, only to be rebuffed. A case in point is Italy, where as early as the 1980s two economists, Paolo Guerrieri and Pier-Carlo Padoan, sought to acquaint their countrymen with the field as it was then developing in the United States. A major conference was convened, featuring a number of leading US academics, followed by an impressive edited volume (Guerrieri and Padoan 1988). However, in the end their initiative proved to have little lasting impact. In Italy, IPE remains largely ignored by all but a few old-line critical theorists in places like the University of Bologna. A rare, more mainstream exception is Manuela Moschella, at the University of Turin, who specializes in the politics of international financial organizations (Moschella 2010).

The most glaring anomaly is France, a country with a long history of political economy going back to the physiocrats of the eighteenth century. Indeed, the links between the pursuit of wealth and the pursuit of power were fixed in French minds as early as the time of Jean-Baptiste Colbert, finance minister to the Sun King, Louis XIV. Yet France has contributed virtually nothing to the modern development of IPE since the field's rebirth after the 1960s. Today only a few hardy souls seek to work in the field, and most of them are not even French. Perhaps best known are Cornelia Woll, a German, and Colin Hay, a Briton, two transplants at the Institute for Political Studies (better known as Sciences-Po) in Paris.

The closest French scholars have come to a distinctive contribution was with the emergence of a so-called "regulation school" in the 1970s, with roots in both classical Marxism and historical institutionalism. Associated primarily with heterodox economists like Michael Aglietta (1976) and Robert Boyer (1990), regulation theory sought to explain how historically specific systems of capitalism are "regularized" – that is, stabilized. Capitalist economies were viewed as a function of complex social and institutional systems. "Modes of regulation" were understood as the sets of laws, norms, and policy regimes that set the context for market activity. However, the regulation school was never able to establish itself as anything more than a niche affair. It certainly failed to generate any broader interest in the study of IPE. More recently Christian Chavagneux (2010), a Frenchman who studied in Britain, tried valiantly to introduce modern IPE to the French academic world, but to no avail.

Why has France been so resistant to joining the invisible college? The best explanation is offered by Jabko (2009), who suggests three reasons. First is the historical French bias against importing any ideas from the despised "Anglo-Saxons" – a cultural aversion that may seem an unfair characterization but cannot be ignored. Many in France, quite obviously, are loath to owe an intellectual debt to the Americans or Brits. Second is the comparativist nature of early regulation theory, which tended to focus attention on the internal dynamics of individual national economies rather than on their international connections. The problematique involved domestic "regimes of accumulation," not the global system. Hence the "international" in political economy was downplayed. Third has been a growing wariness among mainstream French scholars of anything that smacks of Marxist dogma, particularly evident since the 1980s. Rather than risk association with the now disreputable Left, academics interested in economic phenomena have preferred to stick to conventional economics, effectively leaving political economy to become "a scholarly preserve for Marxists," as Jabko (2009: 235) puts it. Others simply have not wanted to touch it.

Connecting the dots

Can the dots be connected? Overall, it is clear that European IPE still lacks visible cohesion. Despite growing interest to be found in a number of locales, the Continent still resembles an archipelago – a series of dots on a map. However, that does not mean that there are no commonalities at all among the islands. In fact, beyond the obvious differences, some points of convergence are becoming increasingly evident.

Admittedly, there remains a great deal of variance in terms of ontology. While many European scholars, particularly in Germany and Switzerland, continue to place the state at the center of analysis in the manner of the American school, others are more than happy to abandon the "shackles of methodological nationalism" in favor of other units of interest. Marxists and critical theorists, along with students of globalization, focus on the world-system as a whole, with a particular emphasis on the forces driving structural transformation over long periods of time. Others concentrate on transnational actors or nonstate agents of various kinds, including multinational corporations, social classes, or nongovernmental organizations. Yet others direct attention to individuals and the collective influence of their behavior on social outcomes – including most notably the group in Denmark promoting the idea of Everyday IPE.

Likewise, much variance can be found in terms of epistemology. Although in some places US-style methodology, with its emphasis on narrow hypothesis testing, would appear to be on the rise, many Europeans still tend to rely most on more qualitative approaches. For some this is a matter of preference; for others, it reflects a lack of sufficient training in more rigorous techniques. Interpretive analysis remains commonplace, particularly among scholars working in the traditions of Marxism, critical theory, or historical institutionalism.

Yet in other respects there is more convergence than at first meets the eye. Most Europeans, including even those most inclined toward an American style of scholarship, see a normative purpose to research. The virtues of positivism are not denied. However, in the spirit of Susan Strange, they take for granted that, ultimately, the question must be addressed: *Cui bono*? Scholars have a responsibility to engage with social issues. Similarly, most Europeans tend be open to a wide range of disciplines beyond economics and political science, including especially history, sociology, and international studies. Unlike orthodox scholars in the United States, they do not feel bound by strict disciplinary borders. Indeed, as indicated, much of the most notable IPE scholarship on the Continent comes from people whose primary affiliation still remains with a variety of other specialties. It is important not to identify Continental IPE only with the kind of work that would pass muster with the US mainstream. Europe's cohort is really much bigger than that. Multidisciplinarity rules.

Perhaps most importantly, there is a great deal of overlap among research agendas across the Continent. Not surprisingly, a disproportionate share of research is devoted to issues of European integration, reflecting the looming presence of the European Union. Much attention also is paid to globalization and related issues of global governance, as well as to issues of international trade and development in the global South.

In broadest perspective, therefore, some of the dots can in fact be connected. Europe's archipelago may remain distant from anything that might be described as a single continent – let alone a single Continental school. Yet the islands are far from isolated from one another, and collectively they do add much value for outsiders. Interest in the field is spreading and new contributions are being made. A lack of cohesion should not be mistaken for a lack of potential.

References

Aglietta, Michel (1976), *A Theory of Capitalist Regulation: The US Experience*, London: Verso.

Altvater, Elmar and Birgit Mahnkopf (1996), *Grenzen der Globalisierung: Ökonomie, Ökologie und Politik in der Weltgesellschaft* [The Limits of Globalization: Economics, Ecology, and Policy in the World Society], Münster: Westfälisches Dampfboot.

Altvater, Elmar and Birgit Mahnkopf (2007), *Konkurrenz für das Empire: Die Zukunft der Europäischen Union in der Globalisierten World* [Competition for the Empire: The Future of the European Union in a Globalized World], Münster: Westfälisches Dampfboot.

Blyth, Mark (2009), "Introduction: IPE as a global conversation," in Mark Blyth (ed.), *Routledge Handbook of International Political Economy (IPE): IPE as a Global Conversation*, London: Routledge, pp. 1–20.

Boyer, Robert (1990), *The Regulation School: A Critical Introduction*, New York: Columbia University Press.

Chavagneux, Christian (2010), *Économie Politique Internationale*, second edition, Paris: Editions La Découverte. [First edition published in 2004.]

Guerrieri, Paolo and Pier-Carlo Padoan (eds) (1988), *The Political Economy of International Cooperation*, London: Croom Helm.

Hobson, John M. and Leonard Seabrooke (eds) (2007), *Everyday Politics of the World Economy*, New York: Cambridge University Press.

Hobson, John M. and Leonard Seabrooke (2009), "Everyday international political economy," in Mark Blyth (ed.), *Routledge Handbook of International Political Economy (IPE): IPE as a Global Conversation*, London: Routledge, pp. 290–306.

Hveem, Helge (1973), "The global dominance system: notes on a theory of global political economy," *Journal of Peace Research*, **10** (4), 319–340.

Hveem, Helge (1996), *Makt og Velferd* [Power and Wealth], Oslo: Universitetsforlaget. [Originally published in Norwegian; published in Swedish in 1997.]

Hveem, Helge (2011), "Pluralist IPE: a view from outside the 'schools,'" in Nicola Phillips and Catherine E. Weaver (eds), *International Political Economy: Debating the Past, Present and Future*, London: Routledge, pp. 169–177.

Hveem, Helge and Carl H. Knutsen (eds) (2012), *Governance and Knowledge*, London: Routledge.

Jabko, Nicolas (2009), "Why IPE is underdeveloped in Continental Europe: a case study of France," in Mark Blyth (ed.), *Routledge Handbook of International*

Political Economy (IPE): IPE as a Global Conversation, London: Routledge, pp. 231–242.

Lütz, Susanne (2002), *Der Staat und die Globalisierung von Finanzmärkten. Regulative Politik in Deutschland, Großbritannien und den USA* [The State and the Globalization of Financial Markets: Regulation Policy in Germany, Great Britain, and the United States], Frankfurt am Main: Campus.

Maliniak, Daniel, Susan Peterson and Michael J. Tierney (2012), *TRIP Around the World: Teaching, Research, and Policy Views of International Relations Faculty in 20 Countries*, Williamsburg, VA: College of William and Mary.

Moschella, Manuela (2010), *Governing Risk: The IMF and Global Financial Crisis*, Basingstoke: Palgrave Macmillan.

Overbeek, Henk (2008), *Rivalität und Ungleiche Entwicklung: Einführung in die Internationale Politik aus der Sicht der Internationalen Politischen Ökonomie* [Rivalry and Unequal Development: Introduction to International Policy from the Viewpoint of International Political Economy], Wiesbaden: VS Verlag.

Pistor, Marcus (2005), "Agency, structure and European integration," in Erik Jones and Amy Verdun (eds), *The Political Economy of European Integration: Theory and Analysis*, London: Routledge, pp. 108–127.

Schirm, Stefan (ed.) (2004), *New Rules for Global Markets: Public and Private Governance in the World Economy*, Basingstoke: Palgrave Macmillan.

Stubbs, Richard and Geoffrey R.D. Underhill (2006), *Political Economy and the Changing Global Order*, third edition, Oxford: Oxford University Press. [First edition published in 1994.]

Underhill, Geoffrey R.D. (2001), *States, Markets, and Governance: Private Interests, the Public Good, and the Democratic Process*, Amsterdam: Vossiuspers.

Van der Pijl, Kees (1984), *The Making of an Atlantic Ruling Class*, London: Verso.

Van der Pijl, Kees (1998), *Transnational Classes and International Relations*, London: Routledge.

7   Latin America

Like Continental Europe, Latin America resembles nothing so much as an archipelago. However, whereas European IPE today can be described as reasonably healthy, a field on the rise, the same cannot be said of Latin American IPE. The story, in fact, is quite different – a tale of lost vitality, a once rich and flourishing field that was then more or less abandoned. Following an early start after World War II, formal work on the politics and economics of international relations actually went into decline, defying trends elsewhere. Across the region as a whole, it became hard to find more than a handful of scholars still committed to IPE as a focal point of inquiry. After a First Generation, there was no Second. Instead, there was a Lost Generation.

Only in recent years has there been some revival of IPE in a scattering of locations around Latin America, from Mexico in the north to Colombia and the ABC nations of the south – Argentina, Brazil, and Chile. Cohorts remain small, however, and relatively isolated. The dots have yet to be connected in any meaningful way. It may be a little unfair to describe the scene as "intellectually barren," as does one recent source (Palma 2009: 243), but it is still fragile and decidedly anemic.

Early contributions

So why include Latin America at all? The reason is simple. Back in the 1950s and 1960s, before the anemia set in, Latin America's contributions to the early development of modern IPE were vigorous and substantial. Principally, these took the form of two interrelated bodies of analysis that came to be known as *structuralist economics* (or economic structuralism) and *dependency theory*. Both approaches were very much in the tradition of historical materialism, in Marx's sense of a materialist conception of history, although neither could be described as classical Marxism. Each provided considerable inspiration for later work in other parts of the globe, including in particular the heterodox scholarship of America's Left-Out and the British school. For a time Latin America was at the creative center of the emerging field of study. The tragedy is that it did not last.

Economic structuralism

The hallmark of economic structuralism, which first emerged in Latin America in the 1950s, was an emphasis on the importance of systemic (structural) features in economic analysis. The central problematique was economic development, a natural preoccupation for Latin Americans conscious of their region's relative economic backwardness at the time. In the decades since, most states in the region have made great progress economically, but in those years, it seemed to many, development could not be addressed without considering the place of individual national economies in the broader system of political and institutional relationships. Structuralist economics focused on internal and external disequilibria arising from the dependent condition of poor countries in the world economy.

Economic structuralism has been described by the noted economist Albert Hirschman as an intellectual breakthrough for the region. Here "for the first time," he wrote, was "a well reasoned, indigenous doctrine" (Hirschman 1965: 282) – a distinctive theoretical model Latin America could call its own. Some have even gone so far as to label it a Latin American "school." An informative retrospective has been provided recently by the Argentine economist Armando Di Filippo (2009).

The name most associated with structural economics was Raúl Prebisch, once governor of the Argentine central bank, who in 1948 was appointed to head the newly created United Nations Economic Commission for Latin America and the Caribbean (ECLAC, also known by its Latin American acronym CEPAL). Others also contributed, such as the Brazilian economist Celso Furtado, who joined ECLAC in 1949 (and later served as a minister in several Brazilian governments), but Prebisch proved most effective in communicating the new perspective to a wider public. As one source comments, "It would overstate the case to term Prebisch the father of structuralism, though he was certainly present at the birth and has since played the role of godfather and high priest" (Jameson 1986: 223).

For structuralists, the starting point was the division of the world economy between a dominant core and a dependent periphery, an idea long central to Marxist analysis (and later to be co-opted by world-systems theory). However, that did not mean that structuralists were Marxists. In a structuralist perspective the central dynamic was derived from fundamental economic characteristics and asymmetries of state power rather than from class warfare or the imperatives of multinational corporations. At issue was the interaction of two interwoven systems, one at the domestic level and one at the international level. The relationship between core and periphery was intrinsic, not a function of global capitalism, and most of the economic problems of the periphery – such as slow growth, inflation, and unemployment – could be directly attributed to specific features of the production structures linking the two tiers. At the center, production was broad and diversified, with a wide range of industrial output. Across the periphery, by contrast, economies were more narrowly specialized in a limited range of commodity exports. Few linkages connected the export sector of a country to the rest of the domestic economy, which consisted mostly of subsistence agriculture. It was these underlying structural differences that were said to account for the lack of development at the periphery.

In effect, structuralist analysis aimed to refute the tenets of traditional theories of international trade. Conventional trade models, going back to David Ricardo and John Stuart Mill, assumed that the "invisible hand" of world markets, promoting resource allocation along lines of comparative advantage, would tend to work to the benefit of all concerned. However, from the beginning structuralists insisted otherwise, anticipating later radical theories of "unequal exchange." The international division of labor, they said, was actually far more one-sided, of much greater value to the core than to the periphery. In these matters, as one source (Palma 2009: 245) has put it, "the 'invisible hand' [is] neither so invisible nor even-handed!"

How did the dynamic work? Here Prebisch made a critical contribution, focusing on the role of the terms of trade (export prices relative to import prices) in the relationship between core and periphery. Over time, he suggested in an influential early study (Prebisch 1950), global demand for the industrial output of the core tended to grow more quickly than demand for commodities, thus depressing the export revenues of the periphery. Being set in competitive world markets, the prices of primary products were typically far more at risk of decline than those of manufactures, which were upheld by a greater degree of monopoly power. Hence over the long run there was a tendency for the terms of trade to turn against poor countries, shifting most of the benefits of exchange to the rich. The presumed tendency toward terms-of-trade deterioration has since become known as the Singer–Prebisch thesis. The label gives equal billing to Hans Singer, a German economist based at the United Nations headquarters in New York, who more or less simultaneously and quite independently came up with the same idea. Both Prebisch and Singer built on earlier musings of the American economist Charles Kindleberger (1943).

The Singer–Prebisch thesis enjoyed a high degree of popularity among development specialists in the 1950s and 1960s, providing what seemed to be decisive justification for the policies of import-substitution industrialization (ISI) that were then being adopted by many developing countries. The disadvantages of the global division of labor, structuralists believed, could be overcome by properly designed measures of amelioration at the domestic level. The fate of the poor was in their hands, not in their stars.

Dependency theory

Yet was that so? For other Latin Americans, reacting to the persistence of poverty in the periphery, the outlook looked grimmer – less amenable to modest reform within the existing capitalist system. In many cases, ISI simply did not work. The model appeared flawed, a failure. Dependency, it seemed, was self-perpetuating, brutally imposed by the prevailing structure of relations and offering no easy escape. Structuralist analysis may have been a useful starting point, a key insight into the role of systemic constraints on the development of national economies, but it failed to appreciate the full power of those constraints in barring improvements in the periphery. Poor countries, in effect, were made poor by the system and forever locked into their poverty. Thus, starting in the late 1950s, was born what came to be known as dependency theory – *teoría de la dependencia*.

Dependency theory, according to one of its leading exponents, could be defined as "an explanation of the economic development of a state in terms of the external influence – political, economic, and cultural – on national development policies" (Sunkel 1969: 23). The approach could be distinguished from economic structuralism in two key respects. First was a difference of disciplinary approaches – their respective intellectual styles. For the most part, structuralism remained bounded by relatively conventional economic constructs. Prebisch, Singer and others may have seemed radical in the eyes of many, but they were trained as economists and spoke the language of their discipline's mainstream. Their concerns, for the most part, were for the typical material objectives of economic policy – growth, employment, and improvements of living standards. *Dependentistas*, by contrast, were prepared to draw upon a much wider range of analytical traditions, ranging from political science and sociology to critical theory and Marxism. Likewise, their goals were more ambitious, aiming not just to put more food on the table but to reinvigorate entire societies. For them, the issue was societal development in the broadest sense of the term, not just production of more goods and services.

Second was a difference of outlook – their respective visions of the future. Structuralists tended to be firm believers in the promise of modernization. Latin Americans and others might find themselves at the periphery of the world economy, but they were not necessarily condemned to remain there. In time poverty could be overcome by a proper mix of policies. For dependency theorists, however, all that was far too sanguine. Inequality was not just an accident of history. Rather, it was intrinsic, an integral product of the periphery's dependent role in the global division of labor. Prevailing capitalist structures systematically deformed local economies and bound them to their fate – the development of underdevelopment, as Andre Gunder Frank (1966) later put it. The poor were not just "behind" or "catching up." Genuine development was categorically impossible within the existing framework of relations. For most *dependentistas* the only solution was socialism, following the example of Fidel Castro's Cuba. Many felt that the collapse of capitalism was inevitable.

Among the earliest contributors to dependency theory was the Brazilian Fernando Henrique Cardoso, a sociologist who later, after a conversion to more conservative views, served two terms as president of Brazil from 1995 to 2003. His early ideas were neatly summarized in a book he co-authored (Cardoso and Faletto 1969). Financial and technological penetration of the periphery by the core, he then argued, produced an unbalanced economic structure that persistently limited self-sustained growth in poor countries. Another important voice was Theotonio dos Santos, also Brazilian, whose perspective was best summarized in a paper delivered to the American Economic Association (AEA) in 1970:

> The dependence of Latin American countries on other countries cannot be overcome without a qualitative change in their internal structures and

external relations ... The relations of dependence to which these countries are subjected conform to a type of international and internal structure which leads them to underdevelopment or more precisely to a dependent structure that deepens and aggravates the fundamental problems of their peoples. (Dos Santos 1970: 231)

Dos Santos also went to great pains to make sure his audience appreciated the difference between *dependentistas* like himself and structuralists like Prebisch and Singer:

In order to understand the system of dependent reproduction and the socioeconomic institutions created by it, we must see it as part of a system ... Attempts to analyze backwardness as a failure to assimilate more advanced models of production or to modernize are nothing more than ideology disguised as science ... The political measures proposed by [structuralists] do not appear to permit destruction of these terrible chains imposed by dependent development. (Dos Santos 1970: 235–236)

Needless to say, Dos Santos's arguments made little headway among the mainstream membership of the AEA. However, among more heterodox scholars in the United States or other countries, the impact of dependency theory was profound, helping greatly to reshape thinking about the challenges of development.

Decline

For IPE scholarship in Latin America, the 1960s were a high point, as the ideas of structuralism and dependency theory were exported around the world. However, after that it was all downhill, as the new field's center of gravity shifted elsewhere. Exit the Lost Generation. Even as the American and British schools emerged in the 1970s and 1980s, soon to be followed by others in the Anglosphere and Continental Europe, contributions from the region largely dried up. In the invisible college that was gradually coalescing, Latin America became an obscure backwater. What caused the decline? Two factors predominated, one political in nature and one economic.

Politically, the environment changed dramatically after the 1960s, following a wave of military coups across the region. Between 1964 and 1990, authoritarian regimes took power in some 11 Latin American nations, including most notably Argentina, Brazil, and Chile. For scholars of a more leftist political persuasion – which of course included many structuralists and *dependentistas* – it suddenly became unsafe to propagate ideas that might find disfavor in government circles. We tend to forget that, in all the other parts of the world where IPE was then on the rise (the Anglosphere, Continental Europe), democracy ruled, allowing for open expression of even the most radical of views. In much of Latin America, by contrast, the same views could land one in jail. You might even be "disappeared." Repression was rife, and in many cases dictatorships simply dismissed troublesome critics or shut down social science departments altogether. Researchers could be forgiven if they felt it wiser to move on to less hazardous pursuits. Some switched to other fields of inquiry. Others, such as Celso Furtado or Theotonio dos Santos, were driven into exile.

Economically, the problem was a growing gap between theory and the facts on the ground. As José Gabriel Palma (2009: 252), a Chilean, puts it, "the complex dialectical process of interaction between beliefs and reality kept breaking down." A strong implication of dependency theory was that capitalism in the periphery could not long survive, given its pernicious effects. The "inevitable" arrival of socialism was only a matter of time. Yet as the years went by, the predicted collapse of the capitalist regime seemed farther and farther away, making a mockery of *dependentista* forecasts. Where was the anticipated revolution? In Palma's words (2009: 252), "A great deal of dependency analysis became like one of those cults that predict the end of the world – in this case, 'the end of capitalism in the periphery is nigh!' . . . The problem with the members of these cults is: what are you supposed to do the day after the predicted doomsday date has passed?" For many scholars in the region, including especially younger academics, the obvious answer was: abandon the theory. Latin America's contributions to IPE went into eclipse.

Revival

Eclipses, however, eventually end – and so too has the decline of IPE in Latin America. Starting in the 1990s, coinciding with a return of democracy to the region, activity in the field has gradually revived. Recovery has been strongest in states big enough to provide the critical mass needed to support the start of a distinct research community, such as Mexico, Colombia, and the ABC nations. However, these are still early days. As in Continental Europe, there is still little cohesion and to date not much that could be described as genuinely distinctive.

Although the outlook appears promising, Latin America is still far from the glory days of the 1950s and 1960, when intellectual breakthroughs were more common.

Factions

Across the region as a whole, the number of scholars who define themselves as specialists in IPE is still relatively small. Again as in Continental Europe, most have been trained in other fields of study and continue to identify themselves mainly in terms of more traditional categories – economics, political science, sociology, and the like. Economists, for example, have hardly lost their taste for addressing public policy issues, but few try to systematically integrate political theories or models into their work. Here too, IPE's low profile was confirmed by the most recent TRIP survey (Maliniak *et al.* 2012: Tables 22 and 23). The results showed that only 3 percent of Argentine respondents specified IPE as their main area of research, as compared with 21 percent who claimed it as a secondary interest. In Colombia, the comparable figures were 4 and 13 percent; in Mexico they were 9 and 16 percent. IPE has yet to come to be treated widely as a separate area of study. For many, it is thought of as little more than a niche speciality at the fringes of academic respectability.

Much more popular are studies of political economy at the *national* level, in the tradition of comparative politics, focusing especially on political institutions and the determinants of public policy. The central problematique remains economic development but emphasizing the internal dynamics of states rather than the links among them. What are the political foundations of foreign economic policy? What are the economic foundations of domestic political regimes? Earlier research explored the links between authoritarianism and economic liberalization (Diaz-Alejandro 1984). Today, not surprisingly given the historical context, particular attention is paid to the relationship between democratization and economic policy. In the pragmatic reforms adopted by ostensibly leftist governments since the return of democracy to the region, many scholars see a new version of structuralism – *neostructuralism* – seeking to successfully combine economic growth, social equity, and representative politics. A useful overview is provided by the Chilean Fernando Ignacio Leiva (2008).

Among those Latin Americans whose work might be identified more as strictly *international* political economy, a cleavage exists between two distinct factions reflecting something of a generation gap. On the one side are scholars, mainly trained in economics or sociology, who strive to preserve the earlier structuralist thinking that was once so dominant in their part of the world. These researchers tend to be proudly radical or "critical" in their perspectives. They also tend to be older, in their 60s and 70s, and their ranks, not surprisingly, are shrinking. On the other side is a growing number of younger scholars, based more in conventional political science, who are seeking to introduce more contemporary perspectives to the region. Many have studied abroad, above all in US universities. Like Canadians, Latin Americans seem divided between an older intellectual tradition and the siren call of a newer American style, including the American school's hard science methodology. Recall the original phrasing of Porfirio Diaz's lament: "Poor Mexico, so far from God, so close to the United States." For Mexico, read Latin America. Regrettably, any dialogue between the two factions is practically nonexistent.

Illustrative of the region's older tradition are the Brazilian José Luis Fiori and the Argentine Mario Rapoport, two influential academics known for their heterodox views on development and global issues. Fiori's thoughts are well expressed in a recent book on *The Myth of the Collapse of American Power*, co-authored with two colleagues (Fiori *et al.* 2008). The perspective of the volume is broadly in the style of historical materialism, with a nod to world-systems theory, and focuses on transformations of international structures at the start of the new millennium. Contemporary crises, they argue, have increased competitive pressures and triggered yet another imperialist race among the great powers. Rapoport's ideas are well laid out in an equally ambitious study entitled *The Grand Crisis of Contemporary Capitalism*, also co-authored (Rapoport and Brenta 2010). The global crisis that started in 2007, the book contends, clearly reveals the flaws of the fragile casino that many "euphemistically" call financial globalization. Such crises are said to be inherent in the dynamics of the capitalist system and always tend to bring with them major social changes and "traumatic" politics.

Works like these, however, are gradually yielding pride of place to a newer generation of scholars determined to join the broader global conversation that began in the United States and Britain in the 1970s. Starting in the 1990s, pioneering classics from the early American and British schools began to make their way onto university reading lists, many in Spanish or Portuguese translations. Among the most popular were works by now familiar names like Gilpin, Keohane, and Strange, highlighting debates over paradigms like realism and liberalism. Soon after that came the first textbooks on IPE, produced by the likes of the Brazilian Reinaldo Gonçalves (2005) and the Chileans Armando Di Filippo and José Miguel Ahumada Franco (2013). Representative of the newer generation is Diana Tussie, an Argentinian, who is widely recognized across the region as a leader in the field. Based at the Latin American School of Social Sciences in Buenos Aires, best known by its Spanish acronym FLACSO, Tussie has pioneered a broad range of studies on international institutions, trade negotiations, Latin American integration, and informal transnational policy networks in the region (Tussie 2003; Riggirozzi and Tussie 2012). She has also been an effective intellectual entrepreneur, having been instrumental in setting up the Latin American Trade Network (LATN), a regional research group.

Apart from Tussie, most of Latin America's newer generation are still too early in their careers to have yet made much of a mark. It is clear, however, that slowly but surely the region is now beginning to catch up with the latest developments in the Anglosphere and Continental Europe.

A Latin American "hybrid"?

Can Latin America regain a prominent place in the greater invisible college? Although as yet the IPE scene remains anemic, there are some glimmers on the horizon to suggest that a brighter future could be in the offing. The dots may yet be reconnected.

The path will not be easy. Across the region barriers to cultivation of a vibrant modern version of IPE are considerable. Language, fortunately, is not among them. With the obvious exception of Brazil, Spanish is spoken virtually everywhere from the Rio Grande to Tierra del Fuego; and even the Brazilians, with their Portuguese, can communicate reasonably well with their hemispheric neighbors. However, other impediments remain to thwart change. Resources to support IPE research are limited. Publishing venues are minimal. Apart from LATN, few professional forums exist to promote debate, and much of the most interesting work in the region never circulates beyond the country in which it originates, leaving cohorts isolated from one another. Worst of all, most university systems — as in much of Europe — are prisoners of tradition, slow to adapt to the birth of new fields of study. Hence, even if a young scholar does aspire to specialize in IPE, few full-time academic positions are available. The headwinds are strong.

Yet despite all that, a range of commonalities has begun to emerge among Latin American scholars that one day could happily converge to define a distinctive new regional version of the field. The degree of within-type variance is declining. Already there is much agreement on matters of ontology, agenda, and purpose. For most researchers the state and public policy generally take center stage. Even among those like Fiori and Rapoport who wish to speculate about broad trends in global capitalism, or others who worry about the implications of globalization, the ultimate goal tends to be state-centric: to bring insight to the problems facing governments and to offer policy guidance to the national authorities. States are the core actors, the central unit of interest. Other factors may enter the picture, but mainly as influences or constraints on decision-makers. The purpose, ultimately, is normative: to redress and improve conditions at the national level. Of course, just as it is for scholars elsewhere – in Australia, Canada, and Europe – the agenda for most Latin Americans understandably is heavily tilted toward the problems of their own nations and region.

The tradition of state-centrism is of long standing. Latin Americans, going back to colonial times, have always expected the state to take a leading role in the management of economic affairs, and scholarship has always had a public purpose. For structuralists, the whole point of analysis was to help countries in the region overcome their economic backwardness. If attention was directed to the broader global division of labor, it was only to better understand what authorities at the state level needed to do – to implement ISI policies, for example. Likewise, for *dependentistas*, the only solution may have been socialism – but socialism in one country at a time, not a Trotskyist world revolution. Hence it was no great leap for a younger generation of scholars to buy into the state-centric paradigm so popular in the United States. Scholarship in the service of the nation seems to come naturally to most Latin American academics. Few seem inclined to throw off the "shackles of methodological nationalism." Even fewer seem to wish to restrict themselves to purely positive analysis.

Similarly, there is also much agreement on matters of epistemology. By a substantial margin, scholars express a preference for traditional qualitative methods over more formal or quantitative analysis. The proportion of regional respondents who listed quantitative analysis as their primary research methodology in the 2012 TRIP survey (Maliniak *et al.* 2012) was mostly in the single digits, comparable to responses from Britain and far below the corresponding share in the United States. As more Latin Americans return to the region after training abroad, a taste for the abstract reductionist style of the mainstream American school is growing, but it is still a minority inclination.

Most importantly, there seems to be growing agreement on what should be the central theme for IPE in Latin America. Since the 1960s, as economic growth has taken off across the region, researchers have lacked a galvanizing idea to inspire a new generation of scholarship. However, consensus is now coalescing around the notion of *autonomy*, seen as an essential precondition for sustaining successful national development. Given the region's long-standing resentment of the dominance of the United States, the *yanqui* colossus of the north, it should not be surprising that scholars might be disproportionately preoccupied with the promise of political and economic independence. Autonomy, after all, is the flip-side of dependency. Even if early structuralist or dependency theories are no longer in favor, ample "policy space" remains a popular goal. In the words of Arlene Tickner (2009: 33), who teaches at the University of the Andes in Colombia, autonomy may be viewed "as a mechanism for guarding against the noxious effects of dependency." What self-respecting Latin American would not want to help promote such a worthy objective? As the perception spreads that US hegemony may now be in terminal decline, Latin Americans are gaining confidence that autonomy may, at long last, actually be within their reach.

The question is: can the theme of autonomy – the antithesis of dependency – be effectively married with some of the more conventional approaches, like realism and liberalism, that are now being imported into the region by a newer generation of scholars? If Latin America is once again to make a distinctive contribution, that would seem to be the way to go. As early as a decade ago, Tickner detected the beginning of just such a fusion in IR scholarship around the region – hinting at the creation of what she called a Latin American "hybrid" model (Tickner 2009: 33). The challenge for today's students of IPE is to patch together a similar hybrid for their own field: to bridge the gap between the heterodoxy of the older generation of structuralists and *dependentistas* and the newer trends currently coming out of the Anglosphere and Continental Europe. For inspiration, researchers might look to Canada, which has successfully managed to produce a cohort of bridge-builders determined to merge seemingly disparate traditions. Latin America could use its own bridge-builders.

References

Cardoso, Fernando H. and Enzo Faletto (1969), *Dependencia y Desarrollo en América Latina*, Mexico City: Siglo XXI Editores. [Later published in English as *Dependency and Development in Latin America*, University of California Press, 1979.]

Diaz-Alejandro, Carlos (1985), "Good-bye financial repression, hello financial crash," *Journal of Development Economics*, **19** (1–2), 1–24.

Di Filippo, Armando (2009), "Latin American structuralism and economic theory," *CEPAL Review*, **98**, 175–196.

Di Filippo, Armando and José Miguel Ahumada Franco (2013), "Economía politica global" [Global Political Economy], in *Manual de Ciencia Politica* [Manual of Political Science], Santiago: RIL Editores.

Dos Santos, Theotonio (1970), "The structure of dependence," *American Economic Review*, **60** (2), 231–236.

Fiori, José Luis, Carlos Medeiros and Franklin Serrano (2008), *O Mito do Colapso do Poder Americanco* [The Myth of the Collapse of American Power], Rio De Janeiro: Record Group.

Frank, Andre Gunder (1966), *The Development of Underdevelopment*, New York: Monthly Review Press.

Gonçalves, Reinaldo (ed.) (2005), *Economía Politica Internacional: Fundamentos Teóricos e as Relações Internacionales do Brasil* [International Political Economy: Theoretical Foundations and Brazil's International Relations], Rio de Janeiro: Elsevier.

Hirschman, Albert O. (1965), *Journeys Toward Progress*, Garden City, NY: Anchor Books.

Jameson, Kenneth P. (1986), "Latin American structuralism: a methodological perspective," *World Development*, **14** (2), 223–232.

Kindleberger, Charles P. (1943), "International Monetary Stabilization," in Seymour Harris (ed.), *Postwar Economic Problems*, New York: McGraw-Hill, pp. 375–395.

Leiva, Fernando Ignacio (2008), *Latin American Neostructuralism: The Contradictions of Post-Neoliberal Development*, Minneapolis, MN: University of Minnesota Press.

Maliniak, Daniel, Susan Peterson and Michael J. Tierney (2012), *TRIP Around the World: Teaching, Research, and Policy Views of International Relations Faculty in 20 Countries*, Williamsburg, VA: College of William and Mary.

Palma, José Gabriel (2009), "Why did the Latin American critical tradition in the social sciences become practically extinct?," in Mark Blyth (ed.), *Routledge Handbook of International Political Economy (IPE): IPE as a Global Conversation*, London: Routledge, pp. 243–265.

Prebisch, Raúl (1950), *The Economic Development of Latin America and its Principal Problems*, New York. [Originally published in Spanish in 1949.]

Rapoport, Mario and Noemi Brenta (2010), *Las Grandes Crisis del Capitalismo Contemporaneo* [The Grand Crisis of Contemporary Capitalism], Buenos Aires: Editorial Le Monde Diplomatique-Capital Intelectual.

Riggirozzi, Pia and Diana Tussie (eds) (2012), *The Rise of Post-Hegemonic Regionalism: The Case of Latin America*, New York: Springer.

Sunkel, Osvaldo (1969), "National development policy and external dependence in Latin America," *Journal of Development Studies*, **6** (1), 23–48.

Tickner, Arlene B. (2009), "Latin America: still policy dependent after all these years?," in Arlene B. Tickner and Ole Wæver (eds), *International Relations Scholarship around the World*, London: Routledge, pp. 32–52.

Tussie, Diana (ed.) (2003), *The Promise and Problems of Trade Negotiations in Latin America*, London: Palgrave Macmillan.

8   China

Finally, we come to China, the modern world's newest economic superpower. Over the decades since 1979, when market reforms first kicked off under the leadership of Deng Xiaoping, the Chinese have achieved one of the most remarkable surges of development in world history – sustaining an average growth rate in excess of 10 percent a year for more than three decades. Not long ago the country was struggling and impoverished, a pale reflection of its once glittering imperial glory. Today China stands as the second largest economy in the world, poised soon to surpass even the United States in total productive capacity. At virtually warp speed, the nation has moved from the periphery to the very core of the global economy, once again warranting its ancient designation as the Middle Kingdom.

Paralleling the country's striking economic rise, interest in IPE has also grown by leaps and bounds, particularly since the 1990s. Swiftly, China has become home to one of the invisible college's larger cohorts of specialists. In not much more than a generation, Chinese IPE scholarship has moved from rigid Marxist dogmas to a far more open and rapidly evolving field of study. As in the case of Latin America, the Middle Kingdom is still catching up with the latest developments coming from the Anglosphere and Continental Europe; here too, scholars have yet to make many distinctive contributions of their own. However, these are still early days, just as they are in Latin America. Research is flourishing, and momentum seems to be building to create a genuinely indigenous version of IPE – a school with, as the saying goes, "Chinese characteristics." However, the jury is still out on whether the effort will succeed.

From Marx to modern

That the study of the world economy in China would once have been dominated by Marxist thought is certainly no surprise. The Communist

Party won the civil war, after all, coming to power in 1949. Under Mao Zedong and his immediate successors, the Beijing government dedicated itself in single-minded fashion to fulfillment of the socialist dream. What does take the breath away is the speed with which all that changed once market reforms began. After some initial resistance, quite understandable under the circumstances, the floodgates were opened to a wave of fresh ideas from abroad. A determined campaign was mounted to bring modern IPE to China.

In an instructive survey, Zhong Fei-teng and Men Hong-hua (2010) outline three phases in the development of Chinese IPE since the start of the reform era. During the first phase, which Zhong and Men suggest lasted until around 1990, classical Marxism still dominated, supplemented by structuralist ideas and dependency theories originating from Latin America. Indeed, political economy for the most part was indistinguishable from Marxist theory *pur et dur*. The prevailing view saw the world economy as an extension of an exploitative capitalist system, divided sharply between an advanced core in Europe, North America, and Japan and a starkly underdeveloped periphery. At the system's peak was the United States, regarded as the dominant – but far from benevolent – hegemon. Below, inherent class contradictions and inter-state conflicts were expected, sooner or later, to bring about the inevitable collapse of capitalism. Although there might be bumps or detours along the way, the road to an eventual socialist victory was assured.

Over the course of the 1980s, however, the first hints of a new view began to appear. In 1981, an Institute of World Economics and Politics (IWEP) was established by one of the central government's leading think tanks, the Chinese Academy of Social Science. IWEP soon began publishing a new journal, *World Economics and Politics*, which provided a convenient venue for experimentation with new concepts and perspectives. *World Economics and Politics* stands today as China's flagship IPE-related journal. Then, following normalization of relations with the United States, translations of some pioneering Western scholarship started to become available, including works by the familiar trio of Gilpin, Keohane, and Strange. Very soon Gilpin's three "models of the future" – the trichotomy of liberalism, Marxism, and realism – came to be widely accepted as a useful template for the emerging field of study in China (Li 2012: 142). Chinese scholars have been making a determined effort to keep up with Western ideas ever since.

The 1990s and first years of the new century saw a second phase, marked by a rapid institutionalization of IPE as a formal field of inquiry. Key was the decision of the Ministry of Education in the mid-1990s to approve IPE as one of the major subjects in the study of international politics and diplomacy. Courses on IPE and related topics, such as transnational organizations and Asia-Pacific economic relations, were quickly introduced into university curricula, and soon indigenous textbooks and other teaching materials began to appear. Although the first IPE textbook to be published (Song and Chen 1999) was heavily weighted toward classical Marxist analysis, with a particular emphasis on historical materialism, others to follow were much more Western in orientation (Chen *et al.* 2001; Fan 2001; Peng 2001). New faculty positions were now to be reserved for specialists in the subject; in some universities full-scale departments of International Political Economy were set up; and scholars across the country were encouraged to explore the more popular theoretical paradigms and methodologies that had been developed in the United States and Britain. New research institutes were established, such as the Peking University Center for International Political Economy Research, which started operations in 2001; and new journals were created to help disseminate research findings. IWEP alone now publishes five widely read periodicals.

Finally, from about 2003 onward, came a third phase, still ongoing, when waves of new scholarly works began to find their way into print on a wide range of topics. Yet more textbooks have appeared – at least six during the new century's first decade alone – and efforts have been made to formalize the development of a broad research network comparable to America's APSA and ISA sections or IPEG in Britain. Since 2010, an International Political Economy Forum sponsored by IWEP and other research institutions has orchestrated a series of annual meetings where Chinese scholars can present and discuss their latest work.

A rapid progression like this, from primitive origins to institutionalization to new waves of research, is by no means unique in contemporary China. Since the beginning of the reform period, similar efforts to modernize scholarship have been promoted across the spectrum of academic disciplines, from the humanities and social sciences to the physical sciences and engineering. However, the achievement is nonetheless striking. In little more than three decades, IPE has managed to become a flourishing field of study in China and an integral part of the globe's greater invisible college. As one recent source (Wang and Pauly 2013) summarizes:

In short, Chinese scholarship in the field changed markedly since the initial period of China's reform and opening up. Compared to the straightforward Marxist–Leninist position of an earlier generation of political economists, contemporary perspectives are much more diverse. Similarities with debates among Western scholars have clearly expanded. In this sense, the most obvious trend is that Chinese scholars of IR and IPE have increasingly been incorporated into the international intellectual community at large.

Today

Enthusiasm for IPE in China today is widespread. A voluminous literature is developing in both the Chinese language and English, pointing eventually toward the emergence of a distinctive new faction in the invisible college. Although scholars have exhibited an admirable openness to all kinds of unfamiliar theories and perspectives, certain commonalities have by now already begun to assert themselves, shaping and channeling research. Surveys of Chinese scholarship find little difference between what is said in Chinese or in English. Gradually, in both languages, a path is being paved to define the Middle Kingdom's preferred approach to the field.

The centrality of the state

Most notable among these commonalities is a nearly universal emphasis on the centrality of the state. The parallel with Latin America in this respect is striking. Like their Latin American counterparts, Chinese scholars seem to have no interest in throwing off the "shackles of methodological nationalism." In the words of a recent commentary by Tianbiao Zhu and Margaret Pearson (2013), the Chinese literature "reflexively favours a strong role for the state . . . and contains a normative presumption that the state is playing, and should continue to play, an important role." Constraints and opportunities for state behavior are explored at length, but the state itself, as a political institution, is rarely subjected to critical analysis. Most scholars simply take for granted that the nation is the key unit of interest. Sovereignty is the main focal point. Implicitly, in line with Chinese tradition, the government is expected to act in the best interests of its citizens.

Moreover, as in Latin America, there appears to be little disagreement about the purpose of IPE research. It is normative: to offer advice to the state – specifically, the Chinese state. The vast majority of Chinese scholarship is unabashedly Sino-centric, driven by a widely shared nationalistic mindset. China is seen as emerging from centuries of decay and humiliation, still seeking to determine its proper place in the world. Scholars see it as their role to help address problems facing the Middle Kingdom at a critical juncture of history. Hence research tends overwhelmingly to be policy-driven. The aim is not to pursue positivist explanations or build theory but, rather, to be "useful" – to serve society. Most work follows a standard two-step format that has been labeled the "challenge–response" mode (Wang 2006a: 364). First a challenge facing the Chinese government is described; then policy recommendations (responses) are offered. Little effort goes into developing a theoretical component to link the two steps. The style is pragmatic and the task is considered to be practical, not conceptual.

Not long ago, when classical Marxism still ruled in the Chinese academy, such an emphasis on the state would have been regarded as an anathema. The proper emphasis was supposed to be on global capitalism, the broad system driven by the dynamics of market competition and class conflict. The core problematique was not national policy but structural change – the never-ending struggle against inequality and exploitation. The state itself was purely derivative, little more than a passive superstructure reflecting the decisive role of the underlying foundation of production relations. However, once scholarship began to open up to Western influences, the dominance of Marxist ideology quickly receded. Although some traces of the old view still remain, perspectives today have clearly shifted in favor of a newer state-centric ontology.

What explains the popularity of state-centered research in China? At least four key factors appear to be involved, which may be conceived in terms of a quartet of concentric circles. First, originating in the outermost circle, is the influence of the earliest translations of Western scholarship that made their way into Chinese universities and textbooks. These included, in particular, Gilpin's three "models," the trichotomy that was so instrumental in shaping early thinking about IPE in the Middle Kingdom. The retreat from Marxism left only liberalism and realism, both variants of a state-centric ontology whose roots extended back to the first days of the American school. For Gilpin, Keohane, and the others of their pioneering generation, all trained in the political-science subspeciality of IR, it seemed only natural to make state policy-making their main concern. Reading the US classics, Chinese scholars were more or less conditioned to think the same way.

In a survey of some 182 articles published in *World Economics and Politics* since the late 1980s, Zhongying Pang and Hongying Wang (2013) find that more than 80 percent of the total rested primarily on Western – mainly American – concepts or theories. Only a minuscule 2 percent, by contrast, sought inspiration in purely China-related sources. The survey was limited to articles on international institutions and global governance. However, there is little reason to think that the sizable sample was not representative of the broader Chinese literature taken as a whole. Given IPE's late start in China, reliance on analytical frameworks already developed elsewhere was quite understandable. Conclude Pang and Wang: "The strong socializing effect of Western IPE scholarship on China . . . is perhaps natural given the short history of IPE in China." This socializing effect has only been reinforced by the increasing numbers of Chinese youth returning to the Middle Kingdom after a period of study in the West.

Second, closer to home, is the influence of a parallel intellectual perspective that originated not in the West but in China's own East Asian neighborhood. That is the idea of the "developmental state," first popularized in the region by the phenomenal recovery of the Japanese economy following the destruction of World War II. Japan seemed to offer a distinctive model of economic management that put a proactive government at the center of the development process, harnessing private market forces to promote economic growth and other public policy goals. Investments and resource allocation could be systematically managed through enlightened regulatory initiatives, fiscal measures, and control of financial resources. For many scholars in East Asia, the idea of the developmental state represented a distinctive contribution to the political economy literature, offering a sharp contrast to the more market-oriented approaches favored in the West. In the words of Walden Bello (2009: 180), a Philippine academic: "If there is one theory or approach that might be said to be uniquely associated with the region, it is the theory of the developmental state." The model was soon adopted by other countries in the region and, ultimately, by China itself. Chinese scholars could not help but be impressed by its relevance to their own nation's conditions and needs. The theoretical underpinnings of the model are rarely questioned. It is simply co-opted as a handy starting point for analysis.

Third, within China, there is the influence of a long-standing cultural tradition, going back to Confucian times, that intellectual activity should not be divorced from public service. The notion of an academic ivory tower – of disinterested "objective" analysis – has little place in the history of the Middle Kingdom. Study was not valued for its own sake. Rather, academics were to be "scholar-officials," fully involved in affairs of state. The desire to be "useful" is built into the society's DNA, passed on from generation to generation for more than two millennia. The best way to honor one's family was to use one's studies to engage in public service. In such a milieu, there is nothing at all alien about falling into a "challenge–response" mode of scholarship. This is another parallel with Latin America.

Finally, within the Chinese academy, there is the influence of practical institutional structure. Virtually all universities and research centers in the Middle Kingdom are state institutions, extensions of the government and ruling party. Universities are run or controlled by the Ministry of Education; most research institutions are attached, directly or indirectly, to different ministries or provincial governments. This means that scholars are, in effect, state employees – not exactly bureaucrats, but certainly understood as public servants. Although there is no tradition of researchers taking temporary positions in government – as there is, for example, in the United States – there is an expectation that they will produce useful advice for policy-makers. All those aspiring to an academic career know that it is their role to contribute to broader policy discussions. Even if they were to prefer otherwise, they would feel constrained to put the state at the center of their research. Their careers depend on it.

Other common features

Two other common features of Chinese IPE relate to the intertwined issues of openness and epistemology. On the one hand, scholars generally appear to be inclined toward the tight disciplinary boundaries of the mainstream US style, which relies on the specialities of economics and political science to the exclusion of most other influences. Yet on the other hand there has been considerable resistance to the demanding hard science model favored by the American school, with its emphasis on positivism and empiricism. Neither broad multidisciplinarity nor rigorous methodology seem to be deemed essential to a "challenge–response" mode of analysis.

Exceptions can be found, of course. According to Pang and Wang (2013), for instance, there is some research in China that does go beyond international economics and IR to incorporate contributions from related specialties like comparative politics and philosophy. This seems to be especially so in studies of the issue of global governance. In their opinion, this puts Chinese IPE "somewhat between the American and British schools" in terms of openness. However, other surveys suggest that the bulk of scholarship in the Middle Kingdom sticks to a much more narrow concept of political economy. According to a recent review by Li Wei (2012), the OEP paradigm of the American school is rapidly emerging as a dominant analytical framework for many Chinese scholars.

Likewise, recent years have seen some movement toward adoption of stricter empirical methodologies, including large-scale quantitative studies. In 2009 a textbook was published devoted exclusively to instruction on the use of formal models and econometrics in IPE analysis (Yu 2009). However, these too remain exceptional. The picture has changed from the field's early years when, as Pang and Wang (2013) put it, "Chinese IPE was characterized by a lack of methodology of any kind." However, scholarship today remains heavily weighted toward qualitative research techniques emphasizing narrative analysis and historical interpretation in the British style. Surveys repeatedly lament the lack of systematic empirical testing in Chinese IPE (Wang 2006b; Li 2012; Song 2011).

Agenda

More diversity prevails when it comes to agenda. The scope of Chinese scholarship is very broad. The range of issues addressed by researchers encompasses everything from the traditional topics of trade and finance to more fashionable questions involving energy, foreign direct investment, or the environment. Yet even here two commonalities are evident.

First, it is plain that the choice of issues is heavily influenced by what happens to be on the mind of policy-makers in Beijing. Monetary questions began to attract attention following the Asian financial crisis of 1997–1998 (Wang and Chin 2013). Likewise, the politics of international trade became a hot topic after China joined the World Trade Organization in 2001. Once it became clear how fully China's economy has come to be integrated into a globalizing world, it was only natural to encourage research on what it all might mean for the Middle Kingdom's national sovereignty or security. Could the Chinese version of a developmental state retain its authoritative role under globalization (Zhu and Pearson 2013)? Would the state's policy independence be compromised by membership in international organizations or by initiatives for global governance (Pang and Wang 2013)? Once it appeared that the hitherto dominant position of the United States in global affairs had begun to slip, it seemed natural to join ongoing debates about the role of hegemony as well (Wang and Pauly 2013). Like scholars in other parts of the world, from Australia and Canada to Continental Europe and Latin America, Chinese researchers tend to display a distinct regional orientation. Whatever the research topic, of most interest is the question of what the issue might mean for China or for the Middle Kingdom's relations with its East Asian neighbors.

Second is what Song Guo-you (2011) calls the "off-China" phenomenon: the tendency of Chinese scholars to direct attention mostly to the political economy of decision-making abroad ("off-China") rather than at home. As knowledge of Western analytical models has grown, much energy has increasingly been devoted to analysis of the role of interests groups or domestic political institutions in the United States or elsewhere – but rarely in China itself, where specialists face formidable obstacles to serious empirical research. The inner workings of government in the Middle Kingdom are not studied in much detail, and there is a remarkable paucity of serious comparative analysis of Chinese and foreign policy-making processes. Partly this is because the decision process in the Middle Kingdom is so notoriously opaque, and partly it is because of the authoritarian nature of the political regime. In the words of Pang and Wang (2013): "First, the policymaking process in China lacks transparency. Despite their semi-official status, Chinese scholars lack access to data . . . Second, many of the empirical issues . . . are still politically sensitive. Understandably, Chinese IPE scholars . . . are reluctant to take on such questions." It is safer to evaluate and criticize the behavior of foreigners.

Tomorrow?

With so many features in common, a distinct research community does seem to be coalescing in China, reinforced by more than a quarter of a century of professional socialization. The field is by now well established and thriving. The question is: what unique contribution, if any, can be expected from IPE scholarship in the Middle Kingdom?

Regrettably, China's new-found enthusiasm for the field has not yet managed to translate into anything that might be described as transformational. Although the level of activity is high, indigenous Chinese scholarship remains at a relatively early stage of the learning curve. IPE in the Middle Kingdom is, in effect, still in its First Generation. Concepts and paradigms are mainly borrowed from elsewhere. Genuine innovation, to date, has been minimal. As Zhu and Pearson (2013) suggest, "scholars have relied heavily on exogenously generated theories . . . they tend to be consumers of theory." In terms of intellectual content, the Middle Kingdom to date has been more student than teacher.

Chinese scholars themselves recognize the challenge. Indeed, many complain bitterly and call loudly for more determined efforts to cultivate an approach they could call their own – an IPE with "Chinese characteristics." A great power like China should not be dependent on the ideas of others, they say. Quite the contrary, China should be a producer of knowledge, just as it is a major producer of goods. A theoretical breakthrough is needed – a fresh perspective more in keeping with the Middle Kingdom's new-found place in the world. Typical is the suggestion of Song Guo-you (2011), who proposes that research should be more "based on China" in order to test whether Western theories can actually explain Chinese experience. Where Western concepts fail, a new analytical framework could be developed to structure and guide scholarship.

The ambition is not unreasonable. Other cohorts elsewhere have their own distinct foundational models, each initially prompted by local conditions or priorities. The American school has its OEP paradigm. America's Left-Out has world-systems theory. The British school has Cox's notion of world orders. Even Latin America would seem to be coming together around a central notion of autonomy, echoing the region's earlier structuralist and dependency theories. So why not China?

What would an IPE with Chinese characteristics look like? For some in China, the key may lie in a re-imagined Confucianism – a return to a range of core values and beliefs that have been a part of Chinese culture ever since the great philosopher Kong Qui (Confucius) walked the earth more than two and a half millennia ago. A movement is afoot to resurrect Confucian ideals for modern times. Central to this Confucian renaissance is the principle of *zhong-yong* – otherwise known as the doctrine of the mean – stressing the virtues of moderation, rectitude, objectivity, sincerity, and honesty. The guiding norm is that one should never act in excess. The emphasis is on ethical conduct and firm rules of propriety. The obligation is expected to apply to states no less than to individuals.

For Chinese students of IPE, therefore, Confucianism would translate into the idea of a "just order" – a benign system of economic relations governed not by force but by morality. Western concepts of international political economy tend to stress the role of hard power and material interests in an environment of anarchy and an ever-present risk of conflict. A Confucian approach, by contrast, would stress "rule by virtue" – leading by moral example – which is more a form of what Western scholars would call "soft" power. Governments would derive their legitimacy, the "mandate of heaven," from upright and able performance, which includes cooperation and fair-dealing. The difference is captured by the notion of *tianxia*, based on an idealized depiction of traditional Chinese statecraft. *Tianxia*, literally "all-under-heaven," envisions a more harmonious world order that transcends petty bickering among states. Peace and prosperity would be sustained through mutual tolerance and moral suasion. The contrast with Western conceptions of the global economy, which take selfishness and acrimony for granted, could not be greater.

It is hard to know, however, how seriously to take all of this. One day, perhaps, the ideals of Confucianism might indeed offer the basis for a new analytical framework. So far, however, the approach exists as little more than a rough sketch – a grab-bag of traditional concepts and ideas. None of it has as yet been fleshed out in formal, systematic fashion. Hence much work remains to be done if ambition is to be converted into accomplishment. Only time will tell whether the idea can actually lead to a distinctively Chinese contribution to modern IPE.

References

Bello, Walden (2009), "State and markets, states versus markets: the developmental state debate as the distinctive East Asian contribution to international political economy," in Mark Blyth (ed.), *Routledge Handbook of International Political Economy (IPE): IPE as a Global Conversation*, London: Routledge, pp. 180–200.

Chen, Yi, Xia Anling and Han Yugui (eds) (2001), *Introduction to International Economics and Politics*, Beijing: High Education Press. [Original in Chinese.]

Fan, Yongming (2001), *Western International Political Economy*, Shanghai: Shanghai Renmin Press. [Original in Chinese.]

Li, Wei (2012), "Development of IPE and its current status in China," *Quarterly Journal of International Politics*, **1**, 138–175. [Original in Chinese.]

Pang, Zhongying and Hongying Wang (2013), "Debating international institutions and global governance: the missing Chinese IPE contribution," *Review of International Political Economy*, **20** (6), in press.

Peng, Peng (2001), *International Political Economy*, Beijing: Social Sciences Academic Press. [Original in Chinese.]

Song, Guo-you (2011), "International political economy based on China: problem domain, theoretical breakthrough and disciplinary integration," *World Economics and Politics*, **1**, 59–76. [Original in Chinese.]

Song, Xinning and Chen Yue (1999), *Introduction to International Political Economy*, Beijing: Renmin University Press. [Original in Chinese.]

Wang, Jun (2006a), "The research on China's sovereignty issue," in Wang Yizhou (ed.), *IR Studies in China, 1995–2005*, Beijing: Peking University Press. [Original in Chinese.]

Wang, Xin and Gregory Chin (2013), "International money and finance in Chinese IPE," *Review of International Political Economy*, **20** (6), in press.

Wang, Yong and Louis Pauly (2013), "Chinese IPE debates on (American) hegemony," *Review of International Political Economy*, **20** (6), in press.

Wang, Zheng-yi (2006b), "Beyond Gilpin's typology of international political economy: IPE and its development in China since 1990," *International Politics Quarterly*, **2**, 22–39. [Original in Chinese.]

Yu, Miaojie (2009), *Political Economy Analysis of International Trade: Models and Econometrics*, Beijing: Peking University Press. [Original in Chinese.]

Zhong, Fei-teng and Men Hong-hua (2010), "IPE discipline in China: a historical analysis," *Teaching and Research*, **6**, 85–93. [Original in Chinese.]

Zhu, Tianbiao and Margaret Pearson (2013), "Globalization and the role of the state: reflections on Chinese international and comparative political economy scholarship," *Review of International Political Economy*, **20** (6), in press.

9 The geography of IPE

After this brisk *tour d'horizon*, from the Anglosphere and Continental Europe to Latin America and China, can anyone deny the diversity of IPE? Words like schizoid, inchoate, or fragmented hardly seem an exaggeration given the remarkable heterogeneity of the field. The invisible college is rent with factions, each with its own priorities and sometimes quite oblivious of what is being said or done by others. Variety reigns.

Amidst such a proliferation of trees, it would seem difficult to make sense of the forest. Yet it is not impossible. A step back does allow us some perspective on the field as a whole – what we may call the geography of IPE. The picture that emerges includes both centrifugal and centripetal forces, influences that divide as well as features that unite. Overall, the geography of IPE resembles nothing so much as the idealistic motto highlighted on the Great Seal of the United States – *E Pluribus unum*, "out of many, one."

The big picture

The big picture is summed up in Table 9.1. The table begins with the five dimensions first outlined in Chapter 1, which I suggested may be considered the most critical points of substance or style that separate one faction from another. These are ontology, agenda, purpose, openness, and epistemology. For each of the nations or regions covered in subsequent chapters, a capsule summary is provided describing the central tendencies of each faction along each dimension. Numerous points of convergence or divergence across the globe may be observed.

Begin again with the American school. The mainstream US version of IPE favors a state-centric ontology and a broad research agenda emphasizing in particular issues of state behavior and system governance. In style it is determinedly positivist, resistant to most disciplines beyond economics and political science, and insistent on a hard science

Table 9.1 The geography of IPE

	Ontology	Agenda	Purpose	Openness	Epistemology
American School	State-centric	State behavior, system governance, US perspective	Positive (explanation)	Mainly economics and political science	Rigorous empirical testing (hard science model)
"Left-Out"	Global system, historical structures	Inequalities, social change	Normative	Broadly inclusive	Qualitative, historical, interpretative
British School	Individuals, states, social forces, historical structures	Very broad	Normative	Broadly inclusive	Qualitative, historical, interpretative
Australia	State-centric	Public policy, Asia-Pacific region	Normative	Inclusive	Qualitative, historical, interpretative
Canada	Both American school and British school (and "bridge-builders")	Both public policy and social change	Normative	Some inclusive	Both quantitative and qualitative
Continental Europe	Individuals, states, nonstate actors, global system	Public policy, European region	Normative	Inclusive	Both quantitative and qualitative
Latin America	State-centric	Public policy, Latin American region	Normative	Inclusive	Qualitative, historical, interpretative
China	State-centric	Public policy, Asian region	Normative	Mainly economics and political science	Mainly qualitative

epistemology. What is striking is how few of these characteristics are shared with other cohorts of scholars, whether located in the United States (the "missing middle" and Left-Out) or elsewhere. Most other discourse coalitions are more normative in tone and more eclectic in analysis, open to insights from a wider range of cognate disciplines. Most also are much less inclined to insist on formal hypotheses or rigorous empirical testing. The gap that I had in mind when I spoke of the transatlantic divide appears, in fact, to be much broader – truly, a kind of *global* divide. It is not just the British who maintain a distance from US orthodoxy. It is just about everyone, with only scattered exceptions. This part of the picture conforms closely with the results of a recent study by Jason Sharman and Catherine Weaver (2013), which concludes that available data "provide ground for skepticism that the 'American school' of IPE does or will define the mainstream."

However, that is not the only divide in the field. Equally striking are the differences between America's Left-Out and the British school, despite their common disdain for the conventions of US orthodoxy. Both camps are normative in aspiration, proud to adopt critical theory's "oppositional frame of mind." Both also are inclusive by preference and reject a hard science approach. Each is much more interested than is the American mainstream in broad issues of systemic transformation and social development. Yet their foundational models differ considerably, drawing inspiration from sharply divergent intellectual traditions. At first glance, world-systems and world orders would appear to share much in common (including that key word "world"). However, to their respective loyalists, the contrasts could not be greater. In Chapter 4, I described the two as first cousins, part of the same family tree – but they are hardly kissing cousins.

Another source of division is Marxism, one of Gilpin's three "models of the future." In some parts of the world, such as Continental Europe or Latin America, as well as in America's Left-Out, the Marxist tradition of historical materialism lives on, continuing to focus attention on the broad dynamics of global capitalism. In other parts of the world, by contrast, including especially the US mainstream, Marxism remains an anathema, to be avoided at all costs. Ironically this has become generally true in China as well, despite the continued rule of a political party that still calls itself communist.

Other lines separate the eclectic British school from more formal work done on the European continent in places like Germany or Switzerland.

Anglophone Canada is sharply divided between US and British influences. Latin Americans are divided between an older Marxist tradition and the newer styles of the American and British schools. In both Latin America and China we see nascent efforts to build versions of the field that have their own distinctive characteristics.

Perhaps the most obvious differences have to do with agenda. Most cohorts, quite understandably, tend first and foremost to be preoccupied with social or policy issues in their own nation or region. Australians write about the Lucky Country and the Pacific. Canadians write about Canada and their giant neighbor to the south. Continental Europeans write about European integration. Latin Americans write about their hemisphere, and Chinese write about the Middle Kingdom and Asia. The biggest exceptions are the American and British schools, where the numbers of scholars are large enough to support a broader research agenda. Yet even in these two factions, scholarship is naturally colored by the perspectives of their respective countries. Much US scholarship, implicitly if not explicitly, is refracted through the lens of America's leadership role in global affairs. Much of British IPE, by contrast, is framed by Britain's experience as a post-imperial power.

Conversely, there are also many points of congruence. Most cohorts see their purpose as, above all, normative – intent, in one way or another, on making the world a better place. Most also embrace multidisciplinarity, enthusiastically incorporating ideas and insights from fields of study beyond economics and political science. And most are proudly tolerant of qualitative or interpretative methodologies, rejecting the reductionist gamble of the American school. Some share an interest in broad historical structures, including America's Left-Out, many in the British school, and a scattering of scholars in Continental Europe and Latin America. Others are happy to retain the "shackles of methodological nationalism," in line with the American school's preference for a more state-centric approach. These include, in particular, factions in Australia, Canada, Latin America, and China. Yet others, such as the Everyday IPE group in Denmark as well as some in Britain and proponents of the "sociological turn" in Australia, make individuals or small groups the primary unit of interest.

On balance, overlaps among factions would seem to be as common as divisions. As conceded at the outset of this *Advanced Introduction*, geographic labels have their limits. Within-type variances are common; between-type variations are frequently blurred. Yet through the thicket of trees a sense of the forest does emerge – a picture of a field that is robust in its variety. On a global scale, IPE is anything but a monoculture.

Connections

Table 9.1 provides a cross-sectional view of the forest as it presently exists. Yet how do the trees connect? Do they grow in splendid isolation, or is there cross-fertilization among them? And to the extent that they do communicate, are their links reciprocal or unilateral? Do some dominate, or is it all a wild and tangled profusion?

Insularity?

Evidence of insularity, in at least some parts of the world, is certainly not lacking. Sadly, that is particularly true of the pre-eminent American school, which for the most part shows little interest in what goes on outside its own ranks. It is not just the Left-Out that are treated with indifference. It is just about any IPE research done anywhere that fails to give priority to the norms of conventional US social science. Marxism is held at arms length. Grand visions of systemic transformation are treated with suspicion. Anything that is not published in English is simply ignored. For the American school, the global divide distancing the US mainstream from others is not a gap to be bridged. Rather, it seems valued more as something of a moat to help defend the purity of positivist analysis. In the words of a senior colleague at one of America's top universities, writing to me in private correspondence, "there really is not much room for discussion . . . There is simply not enough common language, or enough common understanding . . . Conversations across this barrier are essentially fruitless."

For students of international relations, the divide will seem woefully familiar. A comparison with IPE seems apt. As much as three decades ago, political scientists Hayward Alker and Thomas Biersteker (1984) were already documenting what they saw as the parochialism of international relations scholarship in the United States, since corroborated by later studies (Holsti 1985; Wæver 1998; Biersteker 2009). Insularity in American IR is especially evident in the realm of publishing. Little work from outside the United States can be found in US research periodicals. According to the latest TRIP survey (Maliniak *et al.* 2012), more than three-quarters (76 percent) of all articles published in the dozen top IR journals (all but two US-based) over the quarter-century from 1980 to 2007 were written by authors affiliated with US institutions. As Biersteker (2009: 319) summarizes, "Americans tend only to read other Americans."

Moreover, insularity appears to be powerfully reinforced by practices of intellectual reproduction. The same TRIP survey also shows that no more than 5 percent of IR scholars at US universities received their doctorates outside the United States. No other country among the 20 nations included in the survey hires its own PhDs to the same extent as does the United States. Readings assigned in Intro to IR courses in US universities invariably tend to favor home-based authors far more than do course syllabi in any other country, and US scholars are the least inclined to read journals published outside their own country. America's IR students, as a result, remain largely unexposed to intellectual developments elsewhere. Insularity does not necessarily mean absolute isolation, but it does signal a disturbingly high degree of parochialism.

Admittedly, the comparison between IR and IPE may not be perfect. The TRIP project is organized to review the general specialty of international relations as a whole, not international political economy in particular. And as Sharman and Weaver (2013) show, there are some "notable" differences between the overall TRIP poll results and the responses of the subsample of scholars who reported IPE to be their primary or secondary interest. Moreover, as previously conceded, the TRIP sample of publications would appear to include only a "narrow slice" of what reaches print in the United States. Nonetheless, given the close relationship between IR and IPE in the United States, it does not seem unreasonable to consider the survey's IR results to be indicative of general patterns and trends in American IPE as well. Certainly, the data strongly suggest what is most highly prized in US IPE scholarship. The dominance of home-grown work encouraged by the American school leaves relatively little room for exposure to styles or perspectives outside the orthodox US mainstream.

Not that the Americans are alone in this respect. Degrees of insularity in IPE's invisible college persist elsewhere as well, for a variety of reasons. Language barriers, for example, are a constant problem. In Chapter 6 I spoke of the difficulties encountered by Continental Europeans lacking sufficient proficiency in English, the language of the long-established American and British schools. The same impediment obviously handicaps scholars in other areas outside the Anglosphere as well, such as Latin America and China. Physical distance also matters, limiting discourse among factions. For often penurious scholars, unable to afford the luxury of frequent travel, it is difficult to maintain regular dialogue with colleagues in far-flung locales. Most important are processes of professional socialization, which from place to place tend to diverge sharply, reinforcing separate identities.

Yet despite all that keeps them apart, it is clear that the trees are not entirely isolated from one another. Britons talk with Australians and Anglophone Canadians. Continental Europeans and Latin Americans struggle to connect the dots in their respective regions. US publications are translated into Spanish, Portuguese, and Chinese. In the modern age, with all its multiple means of communication, absolute insularity has become relatively rare. Even in the age of the internet, of course, a certain residual level of parochialism may be expected to be found anywhere; national or regional idiosyncrasies are an unavoidable fact of life in a multicultural world. However, the barriers are not totally insurmountable. Cross-fertilization can and does occur.

Hegemony?

Cross-fertilization, however, may take different forms. Are the various cohorts all actively learning from one another? Or is the forest more in the nature of a hierarchy, with one or two species of trees dominating others? In short, are the links among factions reciprocal or unilateral?

Broadly speaking, two polar alternatives may be identified to describe a field of study like IPE. At one extreme would be *diversity*, which IR theorist Kal Holsti long ago formally defined as the "ideal model of a community of scholars" characterized by "reasonably symmetrical flows of information, with 'exporters' of knowledge also being 'importers' from other sources" (Holsti 1985: 13). At the other extreme would be *hegemony*, an invisible college in which the flow of ideas is largely one-way, from one or two central sources (for example, the United States or Britain) to everyone else. The former can be visualized as a balanced network community; the latter, as hub-and-spoke or core–periphery. Which type better approximates the reality of the IPE forest today?

On the face of it, the field would seem to be closer to the model of hegemony, given the prominent place currently occupied by the American school. I once lived near the city of Trenton, New Jersey, an old manufacturing hub where visitors were greeted with a huge sign saying "Trenton Makes, the World Takes." To all appearances, that would seem to be the role played today by the US mainstream in IPE. Whereas the American school is insular, taking few cues from others, scholars elsewhere generally consider it important to keep up with the latest from the United States. For example, few non-US publications show up in US course syllabi. Abroad, however, most reading lists typically include at least a few prominent Americans. Indeed, according to the latest TRIP survey, respondents outside the United States reported that anywhere from 40 to 80 percent of readings in Intro to IR courses were by US authors. While Americans are generally disinclined to read publications from other countries – let alone in other languages – many foreigners feel obligated to stay abreast of US scholarship. Asked about who had produced the best work in IR in the previous 10 years, respondents in the TRIP survey included nine US-based individuals among the top 10 and 17 in the top 20. In all these respects, the flow of ideas from the United States to the rest of the world would appear to be massive. Wæver (1998: 689) calls it "the strange combination of American insularity and hegemony." America makes, the world takes.

Moreover, the American school dominates in terms of sheer muscle, judging by numbers and resources. As noted earlier, as much as half the global IPE community may be resident in the United States (Sharman and Weaver 2013). US universities offer the most jobs in the field. Publishing venues are plentiful, research funding is generous, and professional associations like the American Political Science Association, International Studies Association, and International Political Economy Society offer multiple platforms for the dissemination of scholarship. Location gives US-based scholars a natural advantage in the hurly burly of scholarly discourse.

Yet if this is hegemony, it is a dominance of a very strange sort, given how little emulation we see in actual practice. Ironically, if imitation is the greatest flattery, the American school would appear to be more disregarded than honored. The school, quite appropriately, is accorded respect for its formal theory and systematic methodology. Yet, paradoxically, relatively few scholars elsewhere actively seek to adopt the same demanding style. Although the flow of ideas is largely one-way, the ideas themselves remain largely alien. Most scholars outside the United States – and even the Left-Out inside the United States – reject the abstract positivism of the US mainstream in their own work, preferring more normative, multidisciplinary, and qualitative approaches.

The American school is undoubtedly the most *prominent* – the best known – of all the invisible college's many factions, but prominence does not necessarily translate into practical *influence*.

In personal terms, the irony was brought home to me by some private comments I received while this *Advanced Introduction* was being written from a senior member of the Left-Out. "It is probably not fair to any of us," he wrote, "to say that we are being 'left out' except by many scholars who hold IPE jobs in US political science departments . . . [We] are much more in demand by scholarly colleagues around the world than any of the second generation US mainstream colleagues; we have many more stamps on our passports." When asked why, he replied, "I think that it is more that we focus on questions that are of interest to students and academic colleagues in many parts of the world."

For loyalists of the American school, proud of how much their version of the field has "matured," all this might seem surprising. Do others not recognize the advantages of a stable "normal science," offering both rigor and replicability? When David Lake (2006: 772) first claimed that the OEP paradigm had become a "hegemonic approach", he was careful to make clear that he was speaking mainly of IPE in the United States. However, for many of his like-minded colleagues it seems natural to assume that the style should become hegemonic more widely. The American school provides a clear set of professional standards for others to follow – a guide to what may be considered "good" IPE scholarship. Anything else is of a lesser quality.

However, that too may be seen as evidence of parochialism, if not arrogance. Here too the state of affairs will seem familiar to students of IR. Ever since a landmark article by Stanley Hoffmann (1977) published nearly four decades ago, which famously described IR as "an American social science," it has been evident that, for many American scholars, the US version of IR is the only true version of their specialty – the standard by which all other approaches around the world might be judged. For this sense of superiority they have been rightly criticized as self-centered and myopic, mistaking the particularities of American experience for more universal constructs and verities. In Wæver's words (1998: 726), "American IR scholars are prone to thinking in universalistic categories, but they [need] to be reminded of the cultural specificity of these categories." Echoes Biersteker (2009: 321), "It is important . . . to be able to step outside of the American context and reflect upon how much of what are assumed by many American US scholars to be global, timeless patterns, experiences, or universalizing tendencies are in fact the product of a particular American concern and perspective at a given point in time."

The case has been made with particular force by two non-American political scientists, Arlene Tickner and David Blaney (2012). The pair note the advantages that an early start gave "the West" – by which they mean European as well as US scholars – in setting disciplinary standards for the world as a whole. The study of IR matured earlier in Europe and the United States than elsewhere. Over time, therefore, Western scholars were able to establish the dominance of their own version of the field. Their approach, Western scholars could claim, offered the most general perspective on the specialty. Contributions from anywhere else might be considered as, at best, "particular" or provincial in relation to the presumed universality of Western thought. As the two scholars put it (Tickner and Blaney 2012: 7), "scholarly communities outside the core operate largely in the shadow of an already-existing IR dominated by the West that occupies the top of the disciplinary ladder." Alternative approaches that might challenge orthodoxy could then be dismissed as "unscientific" – or, even worse, ideological. However, since Western thought too may be regarded as particular, growing as it did out of local experience and history, in reality it too can be seen as provincial. That in turn, Tickner and Blaney conclude, invalidates any hegemonic pretensions. As they put it, "exposing the provincialism of (Western) IR undercuts its hegemony and opens space for a plurality of views" (Tickner and Blaney 2012: 3). Even more bluntly, theorists Amitav Acharya and Barry Buzan (2010: 2) declare that "IR theory is in and of itself not inherently Western."

Arguably, much the same can be said about the place of the American school in the modern field of IPE. As more and more factions join the invisible college, adding distinctively new perspectives, the narrowness of US "normal science" is becoming increasingly evident. The point has perhaps been best made by the Briton John M. Hobson (2013) – as it happens, the grandson of the John A. Hobson who was such an important early inspiration for America's Left-Out. In a "critical historiography" of modern IPE, the younger Hobson draws attention to deep "Eurocentric" narratives that underpin orthodox scholarship today. The standards promoted by the American school, he suggests, are really embedded within different variants of Eurocentrism (his label for Western thought). In his words (Hobson 2013): "Rather than being premised on positivist, objective, and universal theories . . . the vast majority of international political economic thought . . . has effectively advanced provincial or parochial normative visions that defend or promote or even celebrate Europe and/or the West as the highest or ideal normative referent in the world political economy." Here too, hegemonic pretensions are undercut.

In fact, the case for the inherent superiority of the American style of IPE is remarkably weak. The US mainstream may have had an early start; it may even have now entered a period of "Kuhnian normalcy." Yet that does not give it the authority to define what is universal in the field and what is not. To pretend otherwise would involve, in the words of geographer John Agnew (2007: 138), "the universalizing of what can be called 'doubtful particularisms.'" The American school deserves the respect it receives. It addresses important problems, is firmly based in theory, and insists on rigorous methodology. However, that does not mean that it necessarily deserves to be privileged above all other factions, which also address important problems and rely on their own theories and methods. Seen in this light, the lack of emulation of the US style is not at all surprising. The Americans may have the muscle. They may even get the lion's share of attention, but that does not make them king of the jungle.

Pluralism

How, then, are we to describe the field? Although a certain amount of insularity is evident, cohorts are hardly isolated from one another. Likewise, although a certain amount of hegemony may exist, there is much less hierarchy than many might have expected. Yet neither do we see the kind of symmetry that matches Holsti's notion of diversity. The previous chapters of this *Advanced Introduction* suggest that, across the globe, lines of communication are mostly open. However, it is also clear that links vary in intensity and are uneven at best. Some countries or regions presently act more as consumers, importing concepts and paradigms from the outside. For now, that is especially the case in areas like Latin America and China, where modern IPE is still relatively new. Conversely, other factions at the moment act more like producers, informing work elsewhere. Obviously, this is true of the American school. It may also be said, to a lesser degree, to be true of the British school, which remains influential in Australia and Canada as well as in parts of Continental Europe. Diversity, in the sense Holsti intended, also fails as a label.

Perhaps the most realistic term would be *pluralism* – a rich cornucopia of competing communities and cohorts. Along similar lines, Anna Leander (2009) of the Copenhagen Business School speaks of "plural stories" or "scientific multiplicity." The key here is to see the connections. Within some factions there may be a danger of an emerging monoculture, with its attendant risks of dessication and diminishing returns. Arguably, this may be particularly true of the American school, as a number of informed observers have suggested. One source alludes to "a certain degree of aridity" in the American style (Farrell and Finnemore 2011: 61); another, more bluntly, accuses the US mainstream of "bizarre herding" into "narrow, myopic" debates (Germain 2011: 88). It could easily happen elsewhere as well. Yet stepping back to take in the forest as a whole, as we do in Table 9.1, it is clear that, amidst the profuse underbrush, varying levels of both openness and influence prevail. The trees are each finding their own way to grow. They are also intertwined. *E pluribus unum*.

References

Acharya, Amitav and Barry Buzan (2010), "Why is there no non-western international relations theory? An introduction," in Amitav Archarya and Barry Buzan (eds), *Non-Western International Relations Theory: Perspectives On and Beyond Asia*, London: Routledge, pp. 1–25.

Agnew, John (2007), "Know-where: geographies of knowledge of world politics," *International Political Sociology*, **1** (2), 138–148.

Alker, Hayward R. and Thomas J. Biersteker (1984), "The dialectics of world order: notes for an archeologist of international savoir faire," *International Studies Quarterly*, **28** (2), 121–142.

Biersteker, Thomas J. (2009), "The parochialism of hegemony: challenges for 'American' international relations," in Arlene B. Tickner and Ole Wæver (eds), *International Relations Scholarship Around the World*, London: Routledge, pp. 308–327.

Farrell, Henry and Martha Finnemore (2011), "Ontology, methodology, and causation in the American school of international political economy," in Nicola Phillips and Catherine E. Weaver (eds), *International Political Economy: Debating the Past, Present and Future*, London: Routledge, pp. 53–63.

Germain, Randall D. (2011), "The 'American school' of IPE? A dissenting view," in Nicola Phillips and Catherine E. Weaver (eds), *International Political Economy: Debating the Past, Present and Future*, London: Routledge, pp. 83–91.

Hobson, John M. (2013), "Part I – revealing the Eurocentric foundations of IPE: a critical historiography of the discipline from the classical to the modern era," *Review of International Political Economy*, **20** (5), in press.

Hoffmann, Stanley (1977), "An American social science: international relations," *Daedalus*, **106** (3), 41–60.

Holsti, Kalevi J. (1985), *The Dividing Discipline: Hegemony and Diversity in International Theory*, Boston, MA: Allen & Unwin.

Lake, David A. (2006), "International political economy: a maturing interdiscipline," in Barry R. Weingast and Donald A. Wittman (eds), *Oxford Handbook of Political Economy*, New York: Oxford University Press, pp. 757–777.

Leander, Anna (2009), "Why we need multiple stories about the global political economy," *Review of International Political Economy*, **16** (2), 321–328.

Maliniak, Daniel, Susan Peterson and Michael J. Tierney (2012), *TRIP Around the World: Teaching, Research, and Policy Views of International Relations Faculty in 20 Countries*, Williamsburg, VA: College of William and Mary.

Sharman, Jason C. and Catherine Weaver (2013), "RIPE, the American school, and diversity in global IPE," *Review of International Political Economy*, **20** (5), in press.

Tickner, Arlene B. and David L. Blaney (2012), "Introduction: thinking difference," in Arlene B. Tickner and David L. Blaney (eds), *Thinking International Relations Differently*, London: Routledge, pp. 1–24.

Wæver, Ole (1998), "The sociology of a not so international discipline: American and European developments in international relations," *International Organization*, **52** (4), 687–727.

10 What have we learned?

So what have we learned? The preceding chapters have revealed a rich and dynamic field of study that is gaining popularity in many parts of the world. Inquiry has been promoted; ideas have proliferated; debates have raged. Yet what is the bottom line – the "take-home message?" After years of toil, what do we know now that we did not know before?

Overall, it may be argued, the message comes in two parts – one having to do with the practical *construction* of IPE, the other having to do with the intellectual *content* of the field. Both are of importance to anyone contemplating further study of the subject.

Construction

Start with construction. What have we learned about how a field of study like IPE is built? Clearly our subject did not spring forth fully developed and eager for battle, like Athena from the forehead of Zeus. In actuality the process was both gradual and hesitant, and in many respects, as the preceding chapters suggest, it is still ongoing. Along the way, a number of useful insights have been gained. Five points, in particular, stand out.

First to note is the absence of a common starting point. IPE is not rooted in a single academic discipline. The field's different factions have converged onto their common interest from a wide variety of professional backgrounds. For the American school the point of departure was the international relations subfield of political science. For America's Left-Out, it was sociology. For the British school it was mostly international studies, which in turn drew from a range of other specialities, including history and law. For many in Continental Europe and Latin America, it was comparative politics or comparative political economy. Is it any wonder, then, that the field today is so diverse? The pluralism of modern IPE goes all the way back to its origins. In effect, multidisciplinarity is written into the field's genes.

Second is the element of contingency – what some might call serendipity. If the stories of IPE in different parts of the world tell us anything, it is that, once factions get started, almost anything can happen. There is no common blueprint for aspiring scholars to follow. Much depends on the unavoidable influence of historical chance. Would the American school have been so preoccupied for so long with hegemonic stability theory had the United States not emerged from World War II as a global leader? Would British scholars have been so resentful of the pretensions of the American school had Britain not been a post-imperial power in decline? Would the Latin Americans have been so concerned about dependency had their region been more successful in attaining self-sustaining development? Would the Chinese be so intent on creating a version of IPE with "Chinese characteristics" had China been less successful as an economic dynamo? Social and historical contexts clearly matter.

Third is the importance of an appropriate infrastructure to support the development of a self-sustaining research community. A "critical mass" of scholars is unlikely to coalesce if jobs or publishing venues are unavailable. Financial support and the institutionalization of professional networks are also of vital importance. The American school, America's Left-Out, and the British school all benefitted from access to professional organizations where study and dialogue could be promoted. Continental Europeans and Latin Americans, by contrast, have been handicapped by a paucity of university positions and inadequate research funding. The rapid development of Chinese IPE has undoubtedly been aided by the central government's commitment to strategic support of the field.

Fourth is the value of an environment that encourages genuine freedom of expression. In the Anglosphere and Continental Europe, scholars could feel free to promote even the most radical of ideas without fear of political reprisal. Critical theory in all its guises could flourish unimpeded; not even Marxism was beyond the pale. IPE, as a result, could blossom and thrive. By contrast, the reverse was true in the Latin America of the 1970s and 1980s, when the military came to power in so many countries. IPE died and was not resurrected until after the return of democracy in the 1990s. It hardly seems a coincidence that the field has as yet notably failed to gain a foothold in many other parts of the world where autocracies still reign, such as Russia, central Asia, and the Arab world. The jury is still out on how the political environment will influence the progress of IPE in China.

Fifth, though by no means least, is the critical role played by professional socialization. The development of IPE in diverse locations is manifestly path-dependent, with each step constraining where the next step will go. The centrifugal forces generated by local practices of intellectual reproduction are difficult to resist. It is hardly surprising to find much evidence of insularity across the field as a whole.

Content

So much for construction. What about content? After so many years, what have we learned in terms of intellectual substance?

Much depends on what we mean by learn. If the achievements of study are to be measured by our ability to make definitive statements about the world around us – to establish firm "social facts" – the level of learning may be rated as negligible at best. The search for universal truths has proved largely fruitless. Even after decades of effort, discord persists over the most basic issues of process and structure. Many theories have been developed, intended to help deepen our understanding of how the world works, but none are universally accepted. An old jibe about the economics profession has it that, if you laid all the economists in the world end to end, you still would not reach agreement. The same, regrettably, may be said of IPE. As Stephen Krasner (1996: 110) ruefully acknowledged in a reflection on the field, explanations "have, in some specific cases, been deeply illuminating, but no one has presented a coherent general theory."

Yet is that the best way to measure learning? Perhaps Gertrude Stein got it right. On her deathbed, surrounded by her closest confidants, the legendary literary figure is reputed to have asked: "What is the answer?" When no one dared to respond, she then added: "In that case, what is the question?" The point is apt. We may not know the answers, but at least we can learn to ask the right questions – to define the substantive content of our inquiry. For many, that is the true test of an academic field like IPE. "I use the term 'political economy,'" Gilpin (1987: 9) once wrote, "simply to indicate a set of questions to be examined." Concurs a more recent source, IPE is best understood as a "question-asking field" (Watson 2005: 15). "The genius of [IPE]," adds a third, "lies in problem posing, rather than problem solving" (Dickins 2006: 480). Students of the subject may never agree on how the world works, but at least it should be possible to agree on how to *study* how the world works.

In effect, that takes us back to the definition of the field with which we started, Gilpin's (1975: 43) "reciprocal and dynamic interaction in international relations of the pursuit of wealth and the pursuit of power." Few students of IPE would disagree with the idea that their subject, in broadest terms, is about the mutually endogenous and ever-changing nexus of interactions between economics and politics beyond the confines of a single state, an amalgam of market studies and political analysis. These are the elements of the world that we want to study – the common denominator of the field.

The devil, of course, is in the details. At the broadest level, we may all accept the same common denominator, but try to get any more specific and differences quickly emerge. Two decades after Strange issued her "Mutual Neglect" manifesto, two of her followers were lamenting that "scholars still debate what exactly should be included in the set of questions that defines IPE" (Murphy and Tooze 1991: 2). As interest in the subject has spread, differences – if anything – have grown even deeper. Across the invisible college as a whole, individuals and factions emphasize entirely distinct sets of questions.

The divergence is best seen in terms of ontology. For some, the central questions involve the *state*. The state, it is assumed, is what makes the world go round. Its policies, therefore, are assumed to define the content of the field. How do we explain public policy? How do we judge public policy? How can we improve public policy? The state, we know, is at the core of how the American school frames study. It is also a principal preoccupation of several other factions of the invisible college, including especially those in Latin America and China. For others, however, IPE is about something more personal – about *people*. It is men and women that make the world go round – individuals and social groupings of all kinds. Civil society, not a political abstraction like the state, defines the field. Questions should focus on human beings as the central unit of interest. That was the perspective preferred by Strange, still followed by many in the British school. It is also the view of a scattering of cohorts elsewhere, such as the Everyday IPE group in Denmark. For yet others, at the opposite extreme, the only proper way to study the world is, in effect, to do nothing less than study the world – the broad structure of the *system* as a whole. Marxists address the evolution of global capitalism. America's Left-Out analyze world-systems. Disciples of Cox speak of world orders. The range of questions could hardly be wider.

Is all that divergence bad? Where some see fragmentation, even chaos, others see an opportunity for productive discourse and debate. None of the units that interest diverse factions around the globe – states, civil society, the global system – would seem, on the face of it, to be irrelevant. All of them would appear to be legitimate objects of study. Nor is there any evident reason to prioritize one ontology over others. The common denominator of a pluralistic field like IPE is – or should be – expansive enough to accommodate them all. The only test is: does the approach meet the basic standards of intellectual inquiry? Do the questions add up to a coherent research program?

The key, as emphasized in Chapter 1, is the degree of communication among the diverse factions. Keohane (2011: 36), looking back to the early years of modern IPE in the United States, recalls the "joyous contestation" of debates involving himself and others of the First Generation of the nascent American school. "Maturation" into a "normal science" was the farthest thing from their minds. What they relished, Keohane remembers, was the "intellectual adventure" of clashing visions – the stimulus of engaged conversation. Every field of study can benefit from a lively competition of ideas.

The challenge for IPE today is to keep that kind of "joyous contestation" alive. The previous chapter spoke of the mix of convergence and divergence in the field. The risk, as I suggested at the outset, is that the balance may be at risk of tipping toward greater insularity as a result of divergent processes of intellectual reproduction. To counter that risk, every effort must be made to build and sustain bridges among IPE's many discourse coalitions. We need more Canadian-style bridge-builders. As Leander (2009: 325) argues, "The coexistence of a multiplicity of scientific approaches is unlikely to leave any trace unless scholars are forced to talk to each other." Another faction's questions cannot be dismissed simply because they are different from our own. Cross-fertilization should be encouraged, not discouraged. We should read one another's work, participate in one another's meetings, and respectfully address one another's scholarship. The field's pluralism should be embraced, not denied.

Above all, the diversity of IPE should be celebrated in the classroom. Instructors should resist the temptation to present just a single version of the field, simply because it is convenient or corresponds to their own priors. Students deserve the whole truth, not just a half-truth. This *Advanced Introduction* offers a start in that direction.

References

Dickins, Amanda (2006), "The evolution of international political economy," *International Affairs*, **82** (3), 479–492.

Gilpin, Robert (1975), *U.S. Power and the Multinational Corporation*, New York: Basic Books.

Gilpin, Robert (1987), *The Political Economy of International Relations*, Princeton, NJ: Princeton University Press.

Keohane, Robert O. (2011), "The old IPE and the new," in Nicola Phillips and Catherine E. Weaver (eds), *International Political Economy: Debating the Past, Present and Future*, London: Routledge, pp. 34–46.

Krasner, Stephen D. (1996), "The accomplishments of international political economy," in Steve Smith, Ken Booth and Marysia Zalewski (eds), *International Theory: Positivism and Beyond*, New York: Cambridge University Press, pp. 108–127.

Leander, Anna (2009), "Why we need multiple stories about the global political economy," *Review of International Political Economy*, **16** (2), 321–328.

Murphy, Craig N. and Roger Tooze (1991), "Getting beyond the 'common sense' of the IPE orthodoxy," in Craig N. Murphy and Roger Tooze (eds), *The New International Political Economy*, Boulder, CO: Lynne Rienner, pp. 11–31.

Watson, Matthew (2005), *Foundations of International Political Economy*, New York: Palgrave Macmillan.

Index